LANDSCAPE AND TOWNSCAPE IN THE SOUTH WEST

LANDSCAPE AND TOWNSCAPE IN THE SOUTH WEST

Edited by Robert Higham

Produced in conjunction with
The Centre for South-Western Historical Studies
University of Exeter

Exeter Studies in History No. 22
University of Exeter

First published in 1989 by
University of Exeter Press
Reed Hall
Streatham Drive
Exeter EX4 4QR
UK

© 1989 Robert Higham and the several authors each in
respect of the paper contributed

A catalogue record for this book is available
from the British Library

ISBN Pbk 9780859893091

EXETER STUDIES IN HISTORY
General Editors: Jonathan Barry and Colin Jones

Contents

The Contributors	vi
List of Illustrations	vii
List of Abbreviations	viii
Acknowledgements	ix

Preface   xi
   Robert Higham

English Uplands, South West and North East: local history and archaeology at inter-regional level.
   (The Harte Lecture, 1987)   1
   Peter Fowler

The development of medieval rural settlement in Somerset   19
   Michael Aston

Peasant farmers, patterns of settlement and *pays*: transformations in the landscapes of Devon and Cornwall during the Later Middle Ages   41
   Harold Fox

New towns for old? Urban reconstruction after fires in the South West: the case of Blandford Forum, Dorset, 1731   75
   Michael Turner

The Georgian landscape garden: Devon in the national context   91
   Steven Pugsley

The reform of urban management and the shaping of Plymouth's mid-Victorian landscape   105
   Mark Brayshay

The Contributors

Peter Fowler has been Professor of Archaeology, University of Newcastle-upon-Tyne, since 1985. He was formerly Secretary to the Royal Commission on the Historical Monuments of England. His interests in the history of landscape in all periods have led him to work widely in Britain, including the South West, and to close involvement with major landowners such as The National Trust and The Forestry Commission.

Michael Aston has been Staff Tutor in Archaeology in the Extra-Mural Department of Bristol University, since 1979. His current interests include the development and decline of rural settlement in the post-Roman period, with special reference to the West Country, as well as monastic archaeology, particularly that of the Carthusian order.

Harold Fox is Senior Lecturer in English Topography in the Department of English Local History, Leicester University. He is currently researching into the manor of Taunton (1200–1347) and on the labouring poor of the Somerset manors of Glastonbury Abbey. His long-term work, of which the essay in this volume is a part, is on settlement and society in Devonshire, A.D. 500–1500.

Michael Turner completed his doctoral thesis at Exeter University in 1984 on provincial urban renewal after fires in pre-industrial England. He is Inspector with the Crown Buildings and Monuments Advisory Group, English Heritage. His current research interests are the architectural development of St. James's Palace, Westminster, and Osborne House, Isle of Wight.

Steven Pugsley, a Devonian and graduate of Exeter University, is currently a postgraduate student at Exeter University. His research topic is the development of the Country House in Devon from 1660 to 1875.

Mark Brayshay, a graduate of Exeter University, is Senior Lecturer in Geography at Plymouth Polytechnic where he specialises in historical geography. His research interests include nineteenth-century emigration from the South West, urban management in the Victorian period, and more recently, local defences of Plymouth in Armada year and the Tudor and Stuart postal system.

List of Illustrations

Fig. 1	Brompton Regis and Upton in the 14th century.
Fig. 2	Brompton Regis in the 17th century.
Fig. 3	Ringworks and Deserted Farmsteads at Bagley and Sweetworthy, Luccombe.
Fig. 4	Somerset—the distribution of certain place-name elements.
Fig. 5	Composite ('polyfocal') village plans in Somerset.
Fig. 6	Selected village plans in Somerset.
Fig. 7	Shapwick—changes in the village plan between 1764 and 1885.
Fig. 8	Batcombe church tower.
Fig. 9	Declining settlement patterns on the manor of Hartland, c. 1365.
Fig. 10	Declining settlement patterns on the manor of Helston in Kirrier, 1337–1486.
Fig. 11	Regional trends in the proportion of land used as arable, c. 1300–c. 1500.
Fig. 12	Crop combinations.
Fig. 13	Tentative examples of movements of cattle.
Fig. 14	Blandford Forum. c. 1731.
Fig. 15	Redevelopment of church and Sheep Market Hill, Blandford Forum, 1731–1760.
Fig. 16	Details of Bastards' House and Red Lion, Blandford Forum.
Fig. 17	Forde Abbey, Thorncombe.
Fig. 18	Mount Edgcumbe, Cremyll.
Fig. 19	Castle Hill, Filleigh.
Fig. 20	Ugbrooke, Chudleigh.
Fig. 21	Endsleigh, Milton Abbot.
Fig. 22	Building density in central Plymouth, 1855–60.
Fig. 23	Plymouth granite paved streets, 1857–1866.
Fig. 24	Plymouth sewered streets, 1860.
Fig. 25	Plymouth street improvements, 1858–1870.
Fig. 26	Plymouth compulsory purchases, 1863–1870.
Fig. 27	Government Sanitary Engineer's Report, 1858.
Fig. 28	Tenders for Hartley Reservoir, Plymouth, 1859.

List of Abbreviations used in Notes

B.L.	British Library
P.R.O.	Public Record Office
D.R.O.	Devon Record Office, Exeter
W.D.R.O.	West Devon Record Office, Plymouth
S.R.O.	Somerset Record Office
C.R.O.	Cornwall Record Office
D.C.O.	Duchy of Cornwall Office
N.Q.	Notes and Queries
Arch.	Archaeological/Archaeology
Hist.	Historical/History
Geog.	Geographical/Geography
Agric.	Agricultural
Rev.	Review
Cal.	Calendar
Econ.	Economic
J.	Journal
Proc.	Proceedings
Trans.	Transactions
Ass.	Association
Inst.	Institute
Nat.	Natural
Soc.	Social/Society
Med.	Medieval
Brit.	British
Dev.	Devon
Corn.	Cornwall
Som.	Somerset

so for example, Trans. Dev. Ass.
Dev. and Corn. N.Q.
Post-Med. Arch.
Med. Arch.
Trans. Inst. Brit. Geog.
Proc. Dev. Arch. Soc.
Proc. Som. Nat. Hist. Soc.
Econ. Hist. Rev.
Agric. Hist. Rev.

Acknowledgements

The contents of this volume were given originally as papers at the second annual Symposium of the Centre for South-Western Historical Studies, held in Exeter in November 1987, before an audience of more than one hundred people. The opening event of the Symposium was the nineteenth Harte Lecture on Local History, given by Peter Fowler, Professor of Archaeology at the University of Newcastle-upon-Tyne. We gratefully acknowledge the assistance of the organizers of the Symposium in the production of this volume, the second of the Centre's issues in the *Exeter Studies in History* series. The Editor would also like to thank Dr. J. Barry for assistance in the final production of this volume.

Fig. 3 based upon work by N. Quinnell; fig. 4 based upon work by Michael Costen; fig. 7 drawn by P. Webb; fig. 8 supplied by J. Bettey; figs. 9—13 drawn by S. Goddard; fig. 22 courtesy of the Ordnance Survey; fig. 16, reproduced from J. Belcher, M. Macartney, *Later Renaissance Architecture in England* (2 vols. 1898-1901, plate LXXXI), supplied by the Department of Geography, Exeter University; fig. 17 reproduced from *Architectural History*, 7 (1964); fig. 19 reproduced from *Country Life*, 85 (1934); fig. 20 reproduced with permission of the West Country Studies Library, Exeter; fig. 27 reproduced courtesy of the Public Record Office. Sources of other plates quoted in their captions; all other figs. are by the authors.

Preface

Historians, archaeologists and geographers have wide-ranging interests. Some of these are so far removed from each other that they represent quite different intellectual frameworks and modes of study. But elsewhere the three disciplines share much common ground, sometimes to the extent that meaningful distinctions between them become blurred. Nothing illustrates this better than the theme of the present volume. Ever since the publication of W.G. Hoskins' *The Making of the English Landscape*, in 1955, all manner of inter-disciplinary research into the origins and development of our rural and urban surroundings has been pursued. In recent years, the South West has benefited greatly from the upsurge of interest in this subject. The resulting work has emphasised not only the intrinsic interest of landscape studies, but also how closely interwoven is the fabric of much of the region's development.

The essays included here do not attempt a uniform coverage of the subject throughout the four south-western counties. They present instead the fruits of recent research in a number of related topics. Peter Fowler examines the similarities and contrasts between the South West and the North East of England, drawing on information from prehistoric to more recent times. His essay reminds us that a major purpose in studying any region is to set it in the context of others. Michael Aston, in Somerset, explores one of the knottiest problems of settlement history, the process by which the medieval settlement pattern came into being. This problem has already been prominent for a century, and will undoubtedly continue to be so. It is vexed by difficult evidence as well as by controversies about the Celtic and Saxon contributions to early culture. Harold Fox, in Devon and Cornwall, looks at an equally challenging topic, the process by which the present settlement pattern emerged out of a period of late medieval change. Even in 'ancient' landscapes such as these, due account must be taken of evolution and the temptation to push everything back to Domesday Book (and beyond) resisted.

Three further essays examine important ingredients of the landscape in more recent times. Ancient though many of the region's smaller towns are, their present appearance frequently owes much to later rebuilding, itself stimulated in several Devon and Dorset examples by destructive fires. Michael Turner looks at urban reconstructions and particularly at what happened to Blandford Forum, Dorset, in the eighteenth century. While much wealth was expressed in urban development, the traditional practice of rural residence in grand houses continued in the countryside. The modern country house became a major component of the landscape, just as the medieval castle had been earlier. Steven Pugsley looks at an integral feature of country houses, their carefully landscaped surrounds and gardens. With reference to Devonian examples, he illustrates how Georgian landscape gardens were part of a wider fashion which gradually lost its French influences, becoming increasingly inspired by less formal notions and by the rise of the professional landscape gardener. Finally, Mark Brayshay examines nineteenth-century Plymouth, explaining how an insanitary and overcrowded city was gradually transformed. The idea of modern town planning can be traced back into the mid-Victorian era, despite our traditional view of that period as one of laissez-faire attitudes.

The contents of this volume arise from the belief that history develops not only from Man's thoughts and actions but also from the physical and cultural environment which he moulds for himself. The essays cover subjects spread across many centuries, in four counties whose boundaries transcend the traditional division between Highland and Lowland Zone. They contain a mixture of rural and urban themes, in a landscape which was created partly 'from below' by the labours of anonymous generations, and partly 'from above' by the conscious decisions of those in authority. Landscape and townscape between them provide a backcloth against which virtually all other aspects of the region's history were worked out.

English Uplands, South West and North East: local history and archaeology at the inter-regional level

(The Harte Lecture 1987)

by Peter Fowler

A belief that 'local attachment ranks among the best feelings of our nature' (Thomas, 1967, 5) is a motivation underlying this essay. It may be a little self-indulgent to compare in public two parts of England I know and enjoy best but behind this realization of an opportunity to share, I hope, a pleasure in the allure of locality, lies a serious intellectual challenge.

The opportunity has been stimulated by the recent publication of two books, Malcolm's Todd's *The South West to AD 1000* (1987) and Nick Higham's *The Northern Counties to AD 1000* (1986). Though both synthesise a great deal and say much that is new, yet each is sufficient unto itself: a history of a region, characterizing it but not defining how it is different from other regions. The South West is not compared with the North, nor *vice versa*. Yet, as the Series blurb observes, 'regional differences are nevertheless very real'. What, in cultural terms, are they? Is there any academic future in comparing the histories, the archaeologies, the local histories of different and spatially separated areas of England, as distinct from only seeking to understand either what happened in each of those areas themselves or how each contributes to some ill-defined 'national history'?

We are all familiar with free-standing studies within a regional framework, a *genre* ranging from the very particular to the regional overview, represented at its best in modern scholarship by such as Thomas' *Camborne*, my predecessor Joyce Youings' *Ralegh's Country* (1986) and, the models for so many of us, Cyril Fox's *Cambridge Region* (1923) and Aileen Fox's *South-West England* (1973). But though there are many histories and historical geographies of regions, syntheses of them at national level, and indeed some comparison of adjacent regions, little intellectual exploration of trans-national comparisons of regions in terms of cultural variety seems to have taken place. Of course it occurs at the descriptive level in the writings of numerous travellers about England from medieval times onwards, and there is no gainsaying the merits of the 'see for yourself' approach. Visual impressions are, after all, stimulating to the mind as well as the eye.

Was it this, I wonder, which, in terms of modern scholarship, stimulated an early observation of inter-regional cultural difference?—and an acute and very formative one too. It concerns a frequent traveller between Exeter, Leicester and Oxford. A book published in 1949 specifically sought, in the editor's words, 'to show you something of the part the West has played in English life, and in return the effect that some of the great events in the nation's history have had upon us down here in the West' (Rowse 1949, 11). It contained a chapter entitled 'The Making of the Landscape' in which its writer and inter-University traveller, one W.G. Hoskins, observed of the Devon landscape that 'there is a landscape of hamlets and isolated farms, not of large, compact villages *like the Midlands*' (my italics). This was six years before Hoskins' classic, *The Making of the English Landscape* (1955), based upon this and similar comparative observations; and fourteen years before his more detailed comparative characterizations of the particular in the 'Highland Zone in Domesday Book' (Hoskins 1963). Even though I do not know 'WG' personally, despite sitting briefly at his feet at Oxford in the mid-50s, in influencing a whole generation of landscape scholarship he has affected me more than most. I hope therefore that, in this Harte Lecture at Exeter, it is particularly appropriate for me to acknowledge the source of many of my aspirations over thirty years.

In using the phrase 'the highland zone', Hoskins was of course himself referring to a 'model' from an earlier generation of geographical scholarship transmuted by Cyril Fox into archaeological terms. That provides part—the respectable part—of my daring to seek some useful comparisons between south-west and north-east England, for both regions lie on the same side, the wrong side in terms of socio-economic prosperity, of the Mackinder/Fox Highland/Lowland division. The 'Uplands' of my title is meant to flag this without actually using the word 'Highland'; for while both the South West and the North East are 'highland' in gross insular terms, perhaps the first comparison to make is that both are similar in that each contains, as every denizen knows, marked internal subdivisions into 'lowland' and 'highland'. Nevertheless, let us not play down the 'highland' topographically: significant areas in each are indeed upland by any British standard—over a thousand feet (*c.* 330m) above O.D. on Dartmoor and Cheviot, for example, and 'highland' in their terrain, geology, flora, fauna and archaeology, as on Bodmin Moor and the north Pennines.

To this we shall return, not least because identification of inter-regional differences and similarities is not itself enough. The real point of the exercise is to see if such comparison helps understanding, both by throwing light from one region to another and more generally at a supra-regional level. It will not have escaped notice, for example, that several of the works listed below (see **Further Reading**), in addition to being good local and/or regional history-cum-archaeology, have a significance beyond the locality—Thomas's *Camborne* in relation to early Christianity in western Britain, for example, and Fox's *Cambridge* as a pioneer in generally applicable method.

Topographically, then, in several respects our two regions are similar. Both are indeed in the 'Highland Zone', with much of their hinterland truly upland; but each has characteristic lowland areas. Examples around some of the south Devon coast have counterparts for about 80 miles in a 10-12 mile wide strip between Middlesbrough and Berwick along the North Sea coast. Both regions have coastlines, penannular in the case of the South West, linear and one-sided in the North East, and culturally significant in each case. Todd remarks (p.1) of the South West that 'the most powerful influence upon the region is the sea. . . . In no other part of England are sea and land so intimately bound together'. This absolute is not true of the North East, though the coast and its estuaries have been and are a major cultural factor there; the difference is that in the North East the hinterland is deeper.

Superficially it might seem that the South West and the North East are markedly similar in that both are at England's extremities; yet this is indeed facile, for the nature of the respective extremes is totally different. The South West is 'real', with a physical boundary between land and sea: it is a peninsula. The North East, in contrast, includes the geographical centre of Britain. It has a land/sea interface on only one side, with only a political boundary between it and 'beyond', a line on a map which has meant very little since the early seventeenth century and is irrelevant to pre-medieval considerations. So, in terms of its land-mass, the North East is distinctly different for, unlike the South West, it is a corridor of communication. Yet, paradoxically, this difference should not be over-emphasized for, precisely because it sticks out into the Atlantic and across North-South sea routes, the South West from prehistoric times was also the way to and from other places, notably Ireland, Atlantic Europe and, later, the New World and then the rest of the world. There lies the difference stemming from the physical location of the two regions. It lies not in extreme positions relative to England but in their positions relative, first, to insular North-South sea-communications, one westerly, the other east coast, and secondly relative to Europe and beyond.

Again probably from prehistoric times, the North East's contacts have been with northern Europe, not the Atlantic fringe, and its 'world vision' has tended to be North Sea littoral-orientated at best rather than the intercontinental horizons of the South West. Of course, many exceptions to both coarse generalizations spring to mind: the export of mining and engineering expertise and hardware from both regions worldwide, for example, is a trait in common. There are quirks too. The export of shipbuilding from Tyneside to Japan nearly a century ago, mirrored by Japanese capital investment in the North East today, forms an unlikely connection on geographical grounds but it reflects a cultural factor—the good reputation of a skilled workforce—and dilutes the force of the crude generalization about regional difference stemming from very different geographical locations.

Such comparative discussion could continue at this very general level but I wish to turn to more specifically historical and archeological matters of inter-regional comparison. The questions are, very simply, how do our regions differ and, if they do, why is this so? To begin with documentary evidence, let us compare these two extracts:

> The reconstructed tenement has a strong claim to represent the original *Cambron* of the eleventh century, if not earlier. Where the original homestead lay is bound to be a matter of some conjecture, but the site of the successive houses called 'Camborne Veor' naturally suggests itself. It is also probable that the Glebe, an irregular area of forty Cornish acres, was detached from the *Cambron* (in the thirteenth century?) to form an endowment for the Rectory by the Bassetts, as owners of the tenement in question and as patrons of the living. (Thomas 1967, 15).
>
> As there is no Domesday Book for Northumberland and Durham, the first mention of Pedam's Oak occurred in the Boldon Book in 1183 ... when Alan Bruntoft held Edmundbyers, including Pedam's Oak, from the Bishop of Durham. Between 1208 and 1217 Alan Bruntoft granted the holding of Pedam's Oak to Master Arnold the earliest known master of Sherburn Hospital. . . . The rent of four shillings, was to be paid at a rate of two shillings twice a year, by the master, and subsequent masters, of the hospital to Bruntoft and his ancestors.
>
> In the fourteenth century, the manor of Edmundbyers was acquired by the Prior and Convent of Durham Cathedral and the rent went to them. These accounts are recorded at Durham under the books for the neighbouring manor of Muggleswick. (Ross 1987, 59).

They make an obvious point but an important one. The two authors are writing of widely-separated areas, and their experience is vastly different, yet both turn to such sparse documentary evidence as is available to achieve the same end, the location of a place, in an implicitly common methodology. Yet to look now at Camborne, Cornwall, and Pedams Oak, Edmundbyers, County Durham, is to see, superficially, two very different places. At the one are the centre and suburbs of a nineteenth century 'boom town', now clinging to the later twentieth century by the tattered fringe of rather tatty tourism; while at the other, high on the eastern moorland flanks of the Northern Pennines, an abandoned farm is surrounded by a patch of upland pasture enclosed within tumbled drystone walls which drop through formerly coppiced but now unmanaged woodland to an undrained valley bottom and its peat-brown burn. The one represents archetypally industrial urban decay, the other agricultural rural decay: different, but with decay in common.

Yet the difference is not a function of their different regional locations. Each has parallels in the other region: for Camborne in the South West read Allenheads in the North East; for Pedam's Oak in the North East read many an abandoned croft high on the moors of the South West. And the similarities, not the differences, are even closer, for despite the totally different appearances of Camborne and Pedam's Oak, in fact the common appearance of decay has, at least in part, a common cause: the decline of England's mining industries in the later nineteenth century in the face of foreign competition. Camborne's prosperity depended on the tin-mining industry: Pedam's Oak viability—it was never prosperous,—depended on the lead-mining industry. A second look at Pedam's landscape shows it to be, less obviously than Camborne's but nevertheless, scarred and heaped with the debris of extractive industry and dotted with the ruinous remains of buildings, chimneys and leets—just like the Camborne area, part of the formerly industrialized South West.

Three points are meant to be conveyed by this specific comparison. The elucidation and writing up of 'history' in apparently very different localities occurs within a common *genre* irrespective of region. Secondly, the particular place, complex and fascinating in itself, can be paralleled historically at a more general level at the other end of the country. And, thirdly, places totally dissimilar in appearance and local position as well as being at opposite ends of the country can share, at a slightly higher level still, a commonality of explanation. Local history as such seldom points these things out; and national history tends to use the Cambornes and the Pedam Oaks to exemplify the general. In fact, I see here not just a two-way flow backwards or forwards between 'national' and 'local' history but three points on an intellectual triangle. The inter-regional side of it—what we might call the Camborne/Pedams Oak axis,—could be as helpful in understanding English history in the widest sense as the interplay between national and local on the other sides.

In neither the South West nor the North East is early documentary evidence plentiful and there are differences in the nature of what survives. The North East, containing an alien imperial frontier, possesses much inscribed Latin from the early centuries AD. Though much of it has been found genuinely *in situ*, it can hardly be claimed that much of it is indigenous in inspiration and, of course, none of it is in a local language. Nevertheless, it tells of many specifics in the North East—builders, dates of buildings, visitors willing and otherwise—and not least about one of its great structures, Hadrian's Wall. The South West has little of this, though it certainly had some of the military, and presumably of the bureaucracy, which created it. Though in Latin, some inscriptions in the North East record native names of gods and goddesses, and the Vindolanda writings, on tablets not of stone, give domestic insights albeit in a military context.

This mention of a relative aspect of the early written evidence in the South West and the North East illustrates one of my introductory points: that the nature of the material reflects the nature of the regions, in this case the differences between a south west peninsula going, in Roman terms, nowhere, and a northern military zone somewhat arbitrarily cutting off 'within' from the land and peoples known to exist 'beyond'. The frontier nature of the North East is of course a recurrent theme, indeed a *leitmotiv* in the region's history and cultural development.

If we stay with literary evidence but move a little later, a major cultural difference becomes apparent. Both areas became Christian, but the sources for the change were different and this is reflected in the evidence. In the South West, inscriptions, often in ogham etched on to the corners of standing stones, and, for a period, a Christianity stemming from western and insular traditions manifested in eremetic monasticism; in the North East, a Christianity introduced from Rome and Canterbury, adopted at the regal apex of society, and based on communal and ordered monasticism using Latin.

The contrast was not, however, so stark for of course early Northumbria in its seventh-eighth century 'Golden Age' was also strongly influenced from the west, exemplified religiously and artistically by the Lindisfarne Gospels. As far as I know, the South West has produced nothing comparable. Yet, despite these different traditions and developments, in the major field monuments of the next centuries, the standing stone crosses, the mainstream of the same Christian religion expresses itself similarly in the two regions. Of course, many differences of artistic detail occur in the crosses' decoration and symbolism, but then again—and this also affects their art—there is a further difference in the ninth and tenth centuries. Then, Northumbria, unlike the South West, was fairly drastically affected by the Vikings.

We begin to see differences, obvious so far, and, more importantly, why those regional differences exist. Take another class of stone artistry in the field. One of the great glories—and mysteries,—of Northumbrian field archaeology is the petroglyphs: hundreds of examples of 'decorations' on living rock, most of them on sandstone in the uplands. Undated but generally regarded as of the Bronze Age, their artistic style surely allows thoughts now of an earlier horizon comparable to that of the 'megalithic art' on the passage graves of the Boyne in Ireland in the mid-third millennium. Be that as it may, portable examples seem to occur performing a secondary function when found in Bronze Age and later contexts such as burial cairns. Occasionally, portable examples of 'rock art' have been found in the South West in cairns but the south-west uplands, notably Exmoor, Dartmoor and Bodmin Moor, apparently lack this type of evidence, a marked contrast with the moors of the North East. In this case, deep in prehistory, no ready explanation presents itself: we can but note the difference.

Such a difference is even more frustrating of our understanding when we note two broadly contemporary similarities in the archaeological record. Beaker pottery is well represented in the South West and in the North East and, without going into whatever is its currently fashionable classification, its common presence begs basic questions. Are we, for example, observing in geographically separate areas merely the manifestations of a supra-regional, indeed international, cultural phenomenon, whatever the mechanics of its distribution; or are we looking at the local products of similar developments in already distinct cultural regions?

Many of the Northumbrian beakers come from, indeed have survived precisely because of the local custom of, unmounded cist burials. Examples still turn up during ploughing; yet, in contrast, such burials, neither singly nor in flat cemeteries, do not characterise the South West. To add to this funereal *mélange* at the inter-regional level, the South West and the North East are to the fore among the areas of high density of Bronze Age burial mounds in terms of national distribution. Perhaps this reflects the monumental security provided by the large proportion of marginal land since the first millennium BC in both regions relative to the other parts of England, but nevertheless it indicates an absolute similarity in terms of contemporary cultural behaviour. This observation holds despite the known differences of detail in burial rite and barrow/cairn construction. If more such structures were properly excavated one suspects that an enormous increase in detailed data would be self-cancelling in comparative terms and that a basic similarity would remain.

Since my south-western audience presumably knows well its local archaeology and history, let me pause to select a few of the characteristics of the archaeology of the North East; for I suspect that, whether or not I am comparing like with like, here in Exeter I may well be comparing liked with unknown. Viewed from Camborne, Alnwick is after all well over the Watford horizon (I might add that viewed from Alnwick, *Newcastle* is psychologically far further than its thirty geographical miles). One of the best-known features of the rural landscape in the North East, much beloved by geographers and takers of picturesque snaps, is of course the 'green' village, a rectangular grouping of inward-facing buildings around a relatively large, grassy central area. These are indeed visually outstanding and historically of great interest but should not be allowed to obscure four other characteristics of the existing rural settlement pattern. Many other villages show evidence of a planned layout without necessarily having been 'greened', at least in rectilinear symmetrical fashion; and others are nucleated but without apparent evidence of planning at all. However, in Northumberland especially, the settlement pattern is markedly dispersed, as in much of Devon, with the characteristic form being a hamlet, locally 'steading', consisting of farm-house, hines' cottages, and attendant farm buildings including a byre traditionally end-on to the house. Such isolated groupings are sometimes around an old core, for example a medieval pele-tower or bastle; more often than is known, I suspect, many, especially those on hill tops, perpetuate occupation of the site in Roman-period farmstead or prehistoric enclosure.

In terms of conventional archaeology, however, the landscape of the North East is one of *deserted* medieval settlements. Earthworks of medieval settlement abound: whole 'dead' villages, their earthworks well-preserved and spread over many acres both on the strip of rolling agricultural plateau between coast and upland and in the uplands themselves. Pedams Oak at 1000 ft once had a 'street'; others lie high up the valleys in the Cheviots, totally deserted now, though care has to be exercised in the field to distinguish between the remains of permanent settlement and of temporary sheiling. Often, despite the impressiveness of the earthworks, desertion is not total: in Northumberland, at South Middleton a farm of that name stands at the eastern end of a kilometre of "deserted medieval village" earthworks, while at Welton, the Hall and the Farm stand at the east and the west ends respectively of 500m of similar earthworks. In County Durham, the Royal Commission has recorded such earthworks at a dozen or so deserted sites on the Magnesian Limestone, characteristically with a still-occupied though now isolated house.

Probably even more obvious in the landscape than the settlement earthworks is the rigg and furrow. In large areas of the North East it is widespread in what is now pasture in the lowlands and much more common than has perhaps been realized on the uplands. In the latter case, its visual and, sometimes, chronological analogues are with the ridge and furrow on the moors of the South West, but in the North East we know that rigg and furrow covers a multitude of techniques and phases of cultivation. At one end, strip ploughing with oxen continued in places until relatively recently; at the other, the recent recognition of 'cord-rig' (slight, parallel ridges, often 70-80 cms wide) takes the history of cultivation in terms of visibly surviving field evidence back at least into the first millennium BC. The main point here, however, is that ridge and furrow blankets much of the North East in a visual way uncharacteristic of the South West.

Another landscape characteristic of the North East is perhaps more contentious in comparative terms. Be that as it may, country houses with their adjacent parks and surrounding estates are a marked feature of the countryside. They dominate much of the countryside especially between Newcastle and Berwick, with an 'architectural gem' seemingly every few miles. None are in the outstanding class of Belton (Lincs.) or Kedleston (Derbys.) but from the now derelict Gibside, through Capheaton, Wallington, Hesleyside, Callally and Belford to Ford, to name but a few, is a series of country seats of considerable variety yet of a certain type, proclaiming much about the way things have been, and to a marked extent still are, in the Northumbrian countryside. The word 'feudal' may not be strictly applicable but it conveys the social and visual flavour of a landscape wherein so much is owned by a few and much of the land is farmed by tenants. Architecturally, this division is further marked by another of the North East's rural characteristics, the 'estate village', of which Belsay, Ford and Etal are well-known models of their kind in a landscape where many other villages betray the signs of their estate nature in their situation, form and building types.

Much of the wealth and social status enjoyed by the rural gentry came from industry. The fees of such as John Dobson, who single-handed 'did-over' many of these residences in the early/mid nineteenth century, came by and large not from agricultural rents and demesne farming but from coal and other mineral mining, ship-building, and the growth of chemical, armament and railway industries on Tyneside. Norman Shaw's extravaganza at Cragside for Lord Armstrong, armaments supplier to a world equipping itself for the First World War, was the last in a markedly regional tradition.

The other side of that coin, along the Tyne but also across County Durham and up the Northumberland coast, produced another regional characteristic, one still perpetuated in the region's image. This is the workers' housing. It is terraced in serried ranks along the Tyne valley virtually from Prudhoe to South Shields and from Wylam to Tynemouth; it is also grouped in villages and, in some ways most characteristically, lined in bleak single rows out in what is still the countryside today as it was when they were built. There are of course many parallels for such in the South West, as on the west of Dartmoor and in West Penwith. This is not surprising, given the similar local histories of parts of the two regions in the eighteenth and nineteenth century, nor is the parallelism in the subsequent fate of this phenomenon unexpected. In the coal-mining area of the North East, however, the mid-twentieth century has given us a new type of 'blot' on the landscape in archaeological terms: not just desertion, leaving the settlement remains to decay into a dead yet visible archaeological site, but wholesale and deliberate obliteration.

Even this process comes at different levels. Some mining villages such as Chevington have disappeared totally, obliterated by what was then the National Coal Board; North Seaton at least survives as an archaeological site, even though all the buildings have been demolished, for the roads remain between the strips of weed lending the site the aspect from the air of a deserted medieval town like Winchelsea; and the Choppington I knew in the 1950s is not there either. The space it occupied is now covered by a new pattern of buildings and roads imposed in private development. Another similar indicator is the New Town: Peterlee, Washington, Cramlington and Killingworth, plonked on to green field sites or laid out beside an existing village. This settlement dynamic in the landscape, both destructive and replenishing, accentuated by a superimposed new road pattern, is both a marked characteristic of the North East in itself and a marked difference in comparison with the South West. There, nothing comparable in nature or extent seems to be contributing similarly to what will become the mid/late twentieth century's distinctive horizon in the landscape archaeology of the North East.

This contemporary 'horizon' being created in one generation is, in archaeological terms, perhaps analogous to a rather different-looking baseline stretched across Northumbria's history and landscape some centuries ago. It refers back to one of the region's fundamentals i.e. its position in a frontier zone. However lofty one's disparagement of this factor in cultural terms, the fact is that for two long historical periods—and goodness knows whether the same applied at any earlier time—a north-south political boundary ran east-west across the region. In later prehistory Cheviot does not appear to have been a cultural or political frontier for it was contained within a Votadinian territory perhaps stretching from Forth to Tees, but any cohesion then was split by the creation of an east-west Roman frontier from Tyne to Solway. This has clearly left an horizon, chronologically as well as physically, in the form of Hadrian's Wall and its attendant installations.

This division subsequently broke down and indeed, whatever the reality and details of the politics of the early medieval period in Northumbria, the region then was not a military frontier zone between 'England' and 'Scotland' in the way that it had been in the early centuries AD and was to become again after the Norman conquest. Indeed, at times it stood facing enemies to the south rather than the north. However, its heyday as frontier zone in the traditional North-South sense came again between the twelfth and seventeenth centuries, and occasionally thereafter. This time, however, there was no Wall; rather is the landscape marked, gloriously to us but less glamorously at the time, by dozens of medieval castles, backed up by urban defences where appropriate and, lower down the military and social hierarchy, by numerous other defensive structures. Of these pele-towers and bastles are regionally characteristic, the one a defendable strong-point, the other essentially a farmhouse affording temporary protection.

Of course, the South West contains many castles too. Some were inserted from the east to impose central authority. Others looked, not south or west to enemies beyond, for there were none, but to internal local and regional threats. All the time, to the east, was the 'royal threat', the bugbear of local hegemony throughout the period. This may be far too simplified a generalisation for the high scholarship of peninsular castle studies to bear but nevertheless it enables me to make my other generalization about the plethora of castles in the North East. Of course they reflect the nature of a frontier zone, of the long-lived antagonisms between emergent nation states, at first only formally concluded by the merging of Crowns in 1603. But, as in the South West, where there was no such frontier dispute, these Northumbrian castles were just as much a reflection of the tension between powerful provincials and the Crown, and between powerful provincials themselves, as they were directed against the Scots. What is pertinent to remark, however, is that a state of uncertainty, even continual lawlessness and actual fighting on many occasions, persisted in Anglo-Scots inter-family terms at local level along the political frontier and south into the uplands of Northumberland well into the eighteenth century, aggravated by the Stuart ambitions and further complicated by their religious overtones. Though this had very little to do with the by then domesticated or ruinous castles, even now something of a 'frontiersman mentality' occasionally shows in the psyche of the region, perhaps most obviously in interpretation of the current north/south divide not in terms of us against the Scots as in 'the South' against us.

We see, then, various characteristics of each region, some distinctive, some finding echoes in the other place. A truism, of course, but I still wonder not just why this should be so but about the mechanisms which produce the differences and similarities, not least in the light of the regions' modern and contemporary history here but very superficially and selectively skimmed. I wonder even more whether any gain to historical understanding at national, regional or local level is promoted by a comparative, inter-regional approach. I would like finally therefore to turn to archaeology, selecting some fairly obvious parts of the record for comparison. In general, some similarities come immediately to mind, reflecting in part the Highland Zone nature of the two regions. Despite the depredations of modern land-use, survival of field evidence is remarkably good in extensive patches. Indeed in comparing the

South West and the North East we are comparing, for later prehistory, the two best-preserved areas of England. Yet both regions share a common weakness in the archaeological record: a lack of long stratigraphical sequences. Exeter's, over two millennia, stands out, but it is a regional exception; so too is Newcastle's, currently being pieced together along the Quayside and around the new castle of William I. A 'real' gap between Roman and Norman has, however, not yet been convincingly closed. Hints of urban sequence occur elsewhere, at Berwick, for example, and as yet unrealised potential exists in other towns. Hexham is one such place, though recent excavation was unsatisfactory, and Durham itself can surely produce a longer stratigraphy than has yet been observed. But neither region has so far exemplified a Winchester-type sequence from prehistoric times, nor perhaps will they do so in an urban context.

Are we touching here on one of the significant similarities of the South West and the North East and, perhaps, one of their major characteristics as regions distinguishing them from the rest of England? Neither region is truly urbanized, even today; and much follows from that, and not just the general lack of stratigraphy. Of course, Exeter and Newcastle stand out, rather as does Norwich for East Anglia, as dominant regional capitals which were of national significance in medieval times and, in Newcastle's case, later too. Plymouth and Sunderland, for example, also rose to national importance for various fairly specific functions in post-medieval times, but such are not supported by an urban-based settlement pattern and economy in either region, reflecting Fox's comment long ago that the Highland Zone is marginal in terms of urbanization. This is reflected in the North East as well as in the South West by such as Morpeth, Alnwick, Totnes and Penzance which are indeed recognisably towns but were always small ones and arguably of an essentially local service nature. Some were possibly inflated slightly relative to the region by some special factor, e.g. the Duke of Northumberland's seat at Alnwick, the harbour at Penzance. What it all amounts to is that, Exeter and Newcastle apart—and then not by all that much—both regions did not have big concentrations of population, either absolutely or relative to other urban places, until the eighteenth/nineteenth centuries.

The point about stratigraphy seems to apply also to the countryside, though some caution is necessary. On Dartmoor, for example, radio-carbon dates indicate prehistoric activity in the same area over at least a millennium, and at Milfield similar long-lived occupancy in the later prehistoric millennia is attested. But there is a clear distinction to be drawn here between phases of activity, perhaps continuous, in an area and a physically observable stratigraphic sequence on a rural site as recorded, for example, at Maiden Castle, Dorset, and on gravel complexes along the Middle Thames and the River

Trent. Again, there are exceptions such as Hembury, Carn Brea and, most significantly, Gwithian in the South West, and, in the North East, at Yeavering and potentially at Traprain Law, Lothian (admittedly not quite in the English North East but close by in the Scottish South East and culturally a nodal point in the region's prehistory). Yet in general the great spreads of 'ancient landscapes' on the uplands of the two regions appear to lack a long observable sequence *in situ*, however many structural phases they may prove to contain when examined by excavation. This coarse generalization is so near to being unsupportable, however, that it should soon prove to be incorrect and I hope very much this becomes the case. In the meantime, however, fieldworkers on the uplands will recognise the sense of what I mean.

Down below, both regions are currently enjoying the emergence of archaeological discovery in terrain amenable to air photography. In relation to the rest of England, of course, such terrains, especially river gravels, are not extensive; nor are they in their regions. But, as *loci* of settlement and exploitation, their cultural significance is probably out of all proportion to their relatively small area. This may not be true of Cornwall, but the potential in east Devon is emerging. In the North East, similar potential has appeared along the River Tees, while in Northumberland, where the coastal plain is transected by numerous rivers, the Milfield Basin is already known to be a major area of settlement. Nor is the record limited to prehistoric evidence: early medieval complexes, as at Yeavering on the River Glen and at Thirlings and New Bewick are already known and at least partly excavated. While their counterparts are presumably at Castle Dore and Gwithian in Cornwall, in the North East we are looking at something culturally, socially and morphologically very different. Whatever the British underlay, Yeavering and Thirlings are Anglo-Saxon (more correctly Anglian?) settlements of the sixth/seventh centuries and unlikely to be parallelled in the South West, at least in Cornwall.

The inter-regional difference pinpointed by such a racial distinction is symbolic of a basic difference between the South West and the North East in the sixth—eighth centuries, reflected perhaps in differences still today. Cornwall, for example, may or may not have a good claim to political independence, but the claim can be based on a nationalism reaching back to *pre*-Anglo-Saxon roots. Northumbria may recall its 'Golden Age' and occasionally toy with ideas of separatism, but any slight validity there may be in them has to be specifically Anglo-Saxon. Indeed, whereas Cornish as a language rooted in pre-Anglo-Saxon times is still scholastically preserved, Northumbrian as a dialect still spoken naturally in parts of the countryside is held to embody not just archaic Anglo-Saxon words but pronounciation and structures unconsciously preserving elements from Old English (as well as from the later Scandinavian phase, also linguistically absent from the South West).

Reverting to the archaeological record, I remain puzzled by the difference between the South West and the North East on the uplands in the second and first millennia BC. The nature of the evidence in the South West is now well-known; in research and publication terms, it is probably at least a decade ahead of comparable work in the North East despite the work of Professor George Jobey's 'one-man Royal Commission'. Jobey isolated types and defined typologies among the varieties of field evidence, building up a massive corpus of data and considerable understanding. Essentially this is what Higham synthesises for the North East, rather as Aileen Fox did for the South West in 1973. Meanwhile, of course, the work of Fleming, Wainwright, Johnson, the Royal Commission and others in the South West has moved on not just to find more sites but to elucidate landscape, land-use and social contexts. Some of Jobey's work, and more recently that of Gates, Harding, Burgess, Coggins, Topping, the Royal Commission and others, have moved in the same general direction, but no outline, cohesive regional view has yet emerged comparable to the south western one compounded of Dartmoor, Bodmin Moor, West Penwith and the Isles of Scilly. The fragmentary position in the North East is both summarized and questioned by Burgess (1984). To illustrate one of many points he raises, let me just take one matter—prehistoric fields—playing to the strength of the South West and my own interest in the subject.

In the North East, the very idea of prehistoric fields has until recently hardly been pursued, let alone discussed on the basis of hard evidence (cf Fowler 1983). Yet two developments have begun to fill this lacuna. First, ard-marks have been noted in numerous excavations largely carried out for other purposes, in most cases on Roman military sites. Recently, Adam Welfare sectioned the bank and ditch of a Roman camp at Greenlee Lough specifically to see if the adjacent cord-rig went under the military enclosure; it did, and was related to ard-marks in the surface of the subsoil. During the winter of 1987-8, a major excavation of the Wall complex at Denton Burn, Newcastle, included in its objectives the recovery of ard-marks, and it was successful to the extent of recording several phases of pre-Wall ard-cultivation.

The cord-rig of Greenlee Lough is but one example of the second development, the discovery of surviving, visible evidence on the ground of fields and their cultivation. Fragments of field enclosures around settlements have previously been noted but it was Burgess, backed up by the Northumberland Archaeology Group (continuing the Jobey tradition of work by adult students), and Gates, while Northmumberland Field Officer, who recognized the existence of field systems, particularly in the Cheviots. Yet nowhere so far is there anything closely similar to the extensive systems of the South West. Three cautions must, however, be entered: one, much of Northumbria has still to be searched systematically with field systems in mind; two, a hint of extensive linear land divisions, possibly analogous to the Dartmoor reaves, has been noted in some places, e.g. by Fleming in Swaledale, Topping in the College Valley and myself elsewhere; and third, the cord-rig itself can occur in blocks at angles to one another. Each block may therefore be in a sense a 'field', even though no obvious boundaries now appear around its edges. Indeed, in one case of its recognition, in my own survey on Hartington Moor, a large block of cord-rig appears to be bounded on two sides by slight lynchets.

In one respect too the recognition of cord-rig as a patchily widespread pre-Roman type of upland field-evidence in north-eastern England and southern Scotland bears on another question long-posed by visible remains on the ground. This concerns the so-called strip lynchets or cultivation terraces. Though another paper could now be written about these, let it merely be noted that previous workers have queried whether they are indeed medieval, by analogy with similar terraces in southern England, or earlier. Certainly, however, some terraces and indeed rig itself, other than the tightly-defined cord-rig, can now be seen to be prehistoric. At Elsdon Burn in the Cheviots, for example, strip cultivation is associated with an enclosed prehistoric settlement; at East Stone House in the same area, a similar settlement overlies similar evidence; while near Ingram conventionally medieval broad-rig up and down a slope is intrusive across terraced rig along the contour. After just two years of looking at the Northumbrian evidence on the ground, I am happy to admit the inadequacy of those southern English models and recognise the presence of prehistoric linear cultivation on the uplands of the North East.

It is pleasant to end on a local upbeat, particularly one with implications far beyond the region. Perhaps the element of local pride therein is the less happy face of local attachment being 'among the best feelings in our nature'. Nevertheless, that will be in part the motivation behind another task soon to be completed. Just as Higham's synthesis faces diagonally across the length of England Todd's *South West*—and never the twain shall meet—so at a very different level will Stanier's *Shire County Guide to Cornwall* (1987) face *Northumberland and Newcastle* (1989) in the same series. Both will look similar, each will be complete unto itself, but neither will compare and contrast with the other. At a more serious level, as administrative convenience packages our academic information increasingly at county level in the very necessary Record Offices and Sites and Monuments Records, it is important now and again to step outside the intellectual constraints which a relatively easy method of access to data might unconsciously impose upon our habits of thought. I know that, quite unlike an SMR, this essay has been generalized, superficial and highly selective; but even if it has but suggested that there is a framework for asking useful questions other than on the penny packet principle of discrete units at county and regional level, then it will have been more than just inter-regional self-indulgence.

Acknowledgements

The original lecture was given without notes but with a large number of slides. For the loan of some of the latter, and for stimulating discussion (from which I have probably hijacked some of their ideas), I am grateful to Colin Burgess, Colm O'Brien, Peter Topping and Humphrey Welfare, all colleagues at the Department of Archaeology, University of Newcastle on Tyne. Bob Higham, as editor, has waited patiently while the combination of a silent tape, supposed to have recorded the lecture as given, and a list of slides used was converted into prose via two incompatible word-processors. Any knowledge I have of the South West owes everything, from both friendship and fieldwork, to Charles Thomas, who also chaired the occasion of the Harte lecture, 1987.

Further Reading

I have referenced only the specific quotations since the subjects of this essay are fully discussed, within admirable bibliographical contexts, in the two recent books by Todd and Higham. Further, the essay is unreferenceable in that much of its stems from observations made and impressions gained during the two years immediately before giving the lecture following my return to my native North East. Nevertheless, these titles provided my quotations and, more importantly, provide a background to some of the matters discussed:

Atkinson F., *Life and Tradition in Northumberland and Durham* (1977)
Baker A.R.H. and Butlin R.A. (eds.), *Studies of Field Systems in the British Isles* (1973)
Burgess C.,(l984): ch. 8 in Miket and Burgess below
Fowler P.J., *The Farming of Prehistoric Britain* (1983)
Higham N., *The Northern Counties to AD 1000* (1986)
Higham R.A. (ed.), *Security and Defence in South-West England before 1800* (1987)
Hoskins W.G., *The Making of the English Landscape* (1955)
Hoskins W.G., *Provincial England* (1963)
Miket R. and Burgess C. (eds.), *Between the Walls: essays on the prehistory and history of North Britain* (1984)

Newton R., *The Northumberland Landscape* (1972)
Roberts B.K., *Rural Settlement in Britain* (1977)
Ross C., undergraduate dissertation on Pedams Oak, Dept. of Archaeology, University of Newcastle upon Tyne (1987)
Rowse A.L. (ed.), *The West in English History* (1949)
Thomas C., *Christian Antiquities of Camborne* (1967)
Todd M., *The South West to AD 1000* (1987)

The development of medieval rural settlement in Somerset

by Michael Aston

This article considers current thoughts on the origins and development of rural settlement in medieval Somerset. It is based on a variety of ideas first set down in a series of articles published elsewhere: a general model is offered in an attempt to link together much of this previous research.[1] Some of the new material presented here is based on the research of my colleague Michael Costen and I am grateful to him for allowing me to discuss some of this in advance of his own publications. In this account the traditional explanation for the origin of settlements in the Saxon and medieval periods will be questioned and an alternative model of settlement development suggested.

Even the most casual examination of modern maps will indicate that settlement patterns in Somerset do not readily fit into schemes of village origins based on invading Anglo-Saxons and active colonisation of dense, impenetrable woodland in the Middle Ages. Large nucleated villages, sited singly in parishes and surrounded by a sea of common fields are noticeably rare; there is abundant prehistoric and Roman settlement of the greatest interest and in the post-Roman centuries the county was of more than regional significance.[2]

Research in this country and elsewhere enables us to develop a general model of settlement development for the millennium AD 500 to 1500. This is not the place to review the evidence on which this model is based and the reader is referred to the most recent literature on the subject.[3] Nevertheless several points need to be emphasised as they are particularly relevant to the west country.

Firstly, there was probably great continuity of land use, if not of actual settlement sites, into the post-Roman centuries. This is particularly likely in a county like Somerset, which was a long way from the postulated primary invasion areas of the Anglo-Saxons in southern and eastern England. Secondly, dispersed patterns of farms and hamlets seem to have been more common in many parts of the country in the centuries before the Norman Conquest than was previously thought. Related to this is the probability that villages were relative latecomers to the landscape, not appearing until the tenth century or even later. Then, many of them seem to have originated either as deliberately planted, and probably planned, settlements or as agglomerations of hamlets, joining together following population growth and subsequent planning of new units.

What was essentially an ethnic (or even 'racial') model of settlement origin up until the 1960s has been replaced therefore by a chronological one. In this the differences between various parts of the country, and in microcosm different parts of a county like Somerset, are explained as the result of social and economic changes through time and not as a reflection of the different ethnic make-up of particular groups such as the Celts or Anglo-Saxons. In a similar way, the former model of gradual colonisation of the medieval landscape from primary centres into the surrounding damp and impenetrable forests and marshes, together with the establishment of daughter settlements, now seems to be largely untenable. Environmental archaeological evidence is increasingly showing that such primeval areas had long been cleared; by the beginning of the second millenium BC on the chalklands and limestone areas and other uplands such as Exmoor and in the first millenium BC elsewhere. The landscape of a county like Somerset was clearly open and well developed by the Roman period.[4]

It is now thought that generally there is more significance in the position of a particular place in the local settlement hierarchy at any time than in what the later documents seem to indicate or what is suggested by its place-name. Early estates, the existence or otherwise of royal or ecclesiastical centres and the organisation of the early church through minsters are all now seen as of considerable significance in explaining how settlement patterns developed and changed.[5] It is possible that the only truly village-like settlements were situated at the 'caputs' of such estates and that the subsidiary nature of most other settlements in earlier times directly affected their later fortunes. The problem in most areas is that we have very little idea in detail of what such early centres, or indeed their subsidiary hamlets, looked like in, for example, the eighth, ninth or tenth centuries. The problem is particularly acute in Somerset, where there has never been any rural excavation of an early farm site which has revealed buildings or structures of the period 500 to AD 1000. In contrast, there is a superb Saxon 'caput' at Cheddar, where Philip Rahtz excavated the royal halls built in timber, enabling us to see what one of these earlier centres looked like; even so, we know little of the contemporary settlement at Cheddar, either around the palace or elsewhere in the vicinity.[6]

The Earliest Medieval Settlement Patterns

For convenience we can discuss the earliest medieval patterns of settlement in Somerset in two parts—those in the west of the county and those elsewhere.

Today in the west of the county, on and around Exmoor, the Brendon Hills and the Quantocks, the settlement pattern is predominantly one of scattered farmsteads with only a few hamlets and villages of any size. It is possible to show that much of this pattern was there in the fourteenth century using the 1327 Exchequer Lay Subsidy Returns for the manors in the region and particularly the surnames contained within them.[7] This work is based on the hypothesis that surnames at this time were actually being formed and therefore can be used as a reflection of a taxpayer's place of abode or occupation, or even physical characteristics. Such seems to be the case as example after example from west Somerset shows a high correlation between a manor, with the surnames of its subsidy payers attached, and the modern parish, with the names of the farms within it.

Formerly it was thought that this lay subsidy information indicated a dispersed pattern of farmsteads in the early 14th century. On further examination, however, it seems more likely that at least some of the places, now represented by farmsteads were in fact small hamlets at that time. In the seventeenth century it is certainly possible to show this for Brompton Regis parish, based on the extraordinary document of 1629 which lists the seats in the church 'and to what estates they do belong'. It is also possible to show from the tithe maps of the 1830s and 1840s that there were several holdings in other places in the nineteenth century—at Yearnor in Porlock for example—and the same can be shown from some eighteenth-century surveys. The research of Harold Fox on Devon farmsteads, and particularly the examples from Hartland parish, indicates the likelihood that surviving medieval farmsteads in many cases may well have been hamlets in the early Middle Ages.[8] The process of the growth of a single farmstead into a small hamlet and its subsequent disintegration back to a farmstead, perhaps through several cycles, can be expected to have been a widespread phenomenon as population grew and then declined and as the economic activity of such settlements changed through the Middle Ages.

From the lay subsidy returns for west Somerset manors it can be shown that there are several places indicated by more than one surname, possibly suggesting several farmsteads in a single hamlet, each perhaps occupied by related farmers (figs. 1 and 2). Thus in 1327 we see both Richard Bitelescombe and Robert de Biteliscombe recorded under Brompton Regis for the single farm of Bittescombe in Upton, and Thomas de Upecote, William de

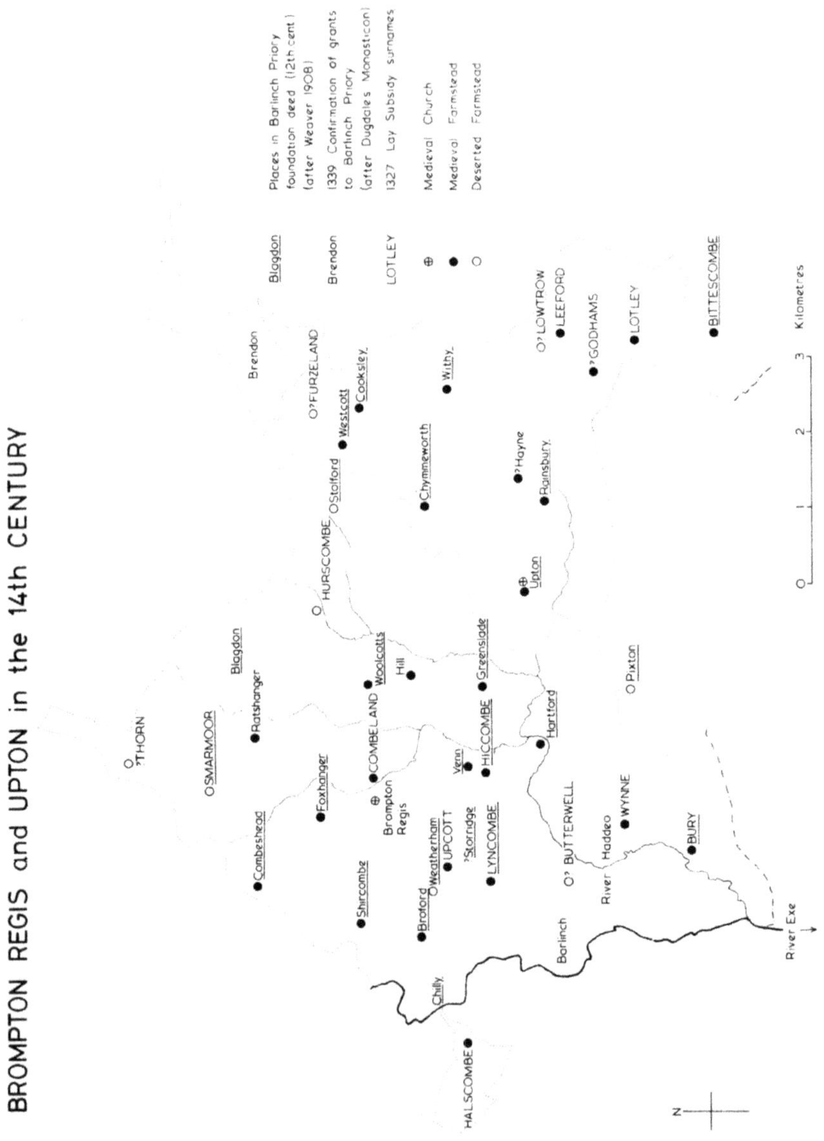

Fig. 1 *Brompton Regis and Upton in the 14th century*

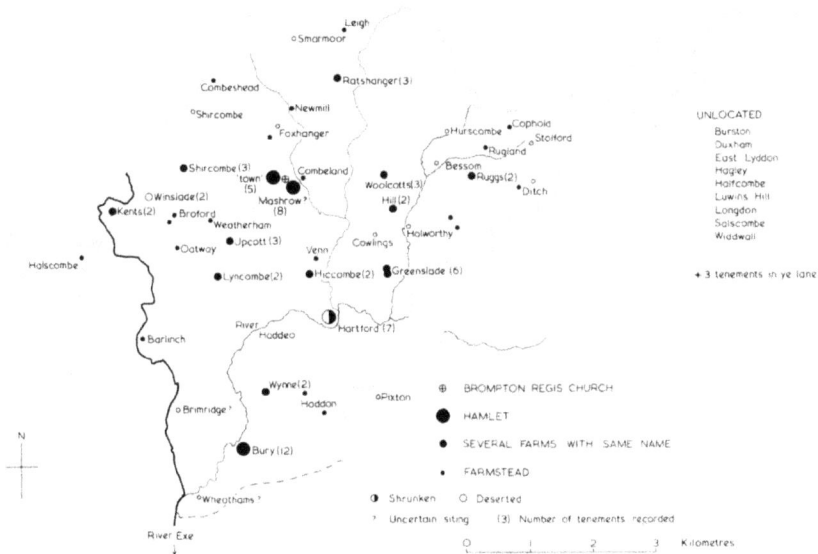

Fig. 2 Brompton Regis in the 17th century

Uppecote and John de Uppecote for Upcott in Brompton Regis.[9] Later records make it clear that the latter was the farm now called Redcross Farm and we also learn from Lord Egremont's estate records and maps (1801–4) of holdings in Upcott called Dawes and Delbridges. A list of 'names of estates' included in the tithe schedule of 1841 includes 'Over Brover'd (Broford) or Dawes' and 'Nether Brover'd or Delbridges', enabling later-named holdings to be linked to earlier recorded farmsteads and suggesting very clearly the former existence of a hamlet rather than a single farm. For Upcott at least it is now possible to suggest that it was a hamlet of three farms in the fourteenth, seventeenth and early nineteenth centuries, although both its name, the tithe map evidence and its present condition show that it has also been a single farm at other times.[10]

Clearly such names are sometimes likely to indicate father and son or some other relationship, while elsewhere two or more names may reflect the possibility of several farms with the same name on different sites. Such may be the case with the three Combes in Brompton Ralph (Combe Davey, Combe Sharney and Northcombe) or Higher and Lower Sowerhill in Brushford with two Sourhulle surnames recorded in 1327. Nevertheless, there must now be a strong presumption that many of the farmsteads in the fourteenth century, apparently recorded in surnames in the lay subsidy, were indeed situated in small hamlets.

Is it possible to say how old these settlements were by the fourteenth century? Susanna Everett argued some time ago that many of these farmsteads were in existence at the time of the Domesday Survey in 1086; in any case, a number were separately assessed as vills at that date.[11] A few of these are deserted, such as Bagley in Luccombe parish, enabling us to see just how small such sites could be. In other areas it is possible to show from documents that some settlements were definitely in existence in the twelfth and thirteenth centuries, if not earlier. For example, the twelfth-century foundation deed for the Augustinian priory at Barlinch lists a number of places in both Brompton Regis and Upton parishes which still exist as farms.[12] Recent research by the editors of the Victoria County History for Somerset on the areas around the Brendon and Quantock Hills has elucidated the medieval history of many extant individual farms and hamlets.[13]

It is likely that many of these early medieval farmsteads may have originated in the pre-conquest period, if not earlier. Several are directly associated with 'ringworks' ('rounds' in Cornwall) and 'hill-slope enclosures' which, elsewhere in the South West, are assumed to be of late prehistoric/Romano-British date. In a few cases the later medieval farmstead is actually situated within such a ringwork; the most obvious examples are Spangate, a deserted farm in Wootton Courtenay parish, and Twitchen in Oare parish. Elsewhere farms of known medieval date are directly associated with ringworks in a way which suggests that the same area of land was being worked over a long period even if the site of the settlement itself has been moved. Such might be the case at Rode (or Road) and Staddon in Winsford parish but the clearest example is at Bagley and Sweetworthy in Luccombe parish (fig. 3).

The prominent earthwork at Sweetworthy has been known for a long time and while it has never been scientifically excavated, it is generally assumed to have been a settlement site of late prehistoric date.[14] Nearby are the remains of the farmstead of Bagley which was still occupied until the nineteenth century but which is also the name of a vill recorded in 1086 in Domesday Book. Both of these sites lie within a large enclosure of improved

Development of medieval rural settlement in Somerset

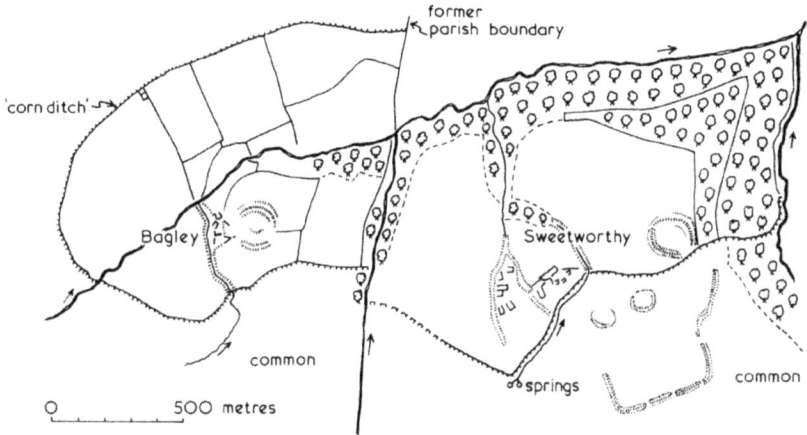

Fig. 3 Ringworks and deserted farmsteads at Bagley and Sweetworthy, Luccombe

land surrounded by a massive stone wall and bank. There is unimproved pasture to the west and south stretching up to Dunkery Beacon; the sites are at a height of 1100 feet on the north side of Exmoor. Recently two additional pieces of evidence have come to light enabling a reappraisal of these apparently unrelated sites. The National Trust, which owns a lot of the land around Dunkery, cleared much of the scrub to the west of Sweetworthy and revealed a previously unknown group of earthworks. These seem to be the remains of longhouses and enclosures and may be the 'Sweetworthy' from which the adjacent enclosure was named. A superb air photograph by John White of West Air Photography shows not only this new settlement site but also several new ringworks. Two of these together with a large embanked area are situated near to the Sweetworthy enclosure but another, unfortunately largely ploughed out, lies immediately to the east of the deserted Bagley farm site.

From two sites existing apparently in isolation we can now see that there are essentially two complexes of farmsteads. One, probably consisting of several ringworks and enclosures in the prehistoric period, has a deserted farmstead whose suggestive name of Sweetworthy contains the Saxon habitative place-name element 'worth'. The other has a badly eroded ringwork with a recently deserted farmstead adjacent, together with the probable remains of a longhouse, and the likelihood is that it is the site of a documented eleventh-century settlement.

This evidence seems to suggest that hamlets and farmsteads were the persistent settlement types in the west of the county from at least the time of the Norman conquest and that the origin of the dispersed pattern of these sites can be assumed to have occurred in the late prehistoric period at the latest. As yet there is little evidence of Saxon or medieval colonisation onto higher or lower land, although such an origin was suggested for the farmstead at Hurscombe in Brompton Regis.[15] However, when so much of the dating of sites is based on the existence or otherwise of pottery and so very little of any single settlement complex has been excavated, it would be rash to make statements which are too definite about the origin of any particular site which has been examined so far.

In east Somerset the situation is somewhat different. This is the part of the county with a predominance of villages and hamlets and, as we shall see, a high incidence of settlement shrinkage and desertion.[16] Much of the land is down to permanent, or almost permanent, pasture making the identification of earlier sites from scatters of potsherds virtually impossible. Some sites have now been recorded from cropmarks but the lack of a local pottery industry before the very late Saxon period means that fieldwalking on ploughed land is not likely to produce much evidence of late Saxon settlements. Thus the methods of locating settlement change in the Saxon and early medieval periods, which have proved so dramatic in parts of the Midlands and the East of England, are denied to fieldworkers in the West of England.[17]

Michael Costen has, however, developed an hypothesis using fieldnames that may well prove to be as useful in locating early settlements in the Somerset landscape as potsherds have been in eastern England.[18] Using field- and place-names derived from Anglo-Saxon charters, medieval documents and the tithe schedules, he has suggested that much of eastern and central Somerset was formerly covered with a dense network of scattered, individually held, farmsteads (fig. 4). Many of these had the elements 'wick', 'worth' or 'worthy', 'cote', 'huish' or 'hewish' or 'croft' in their names indicating some sort of habitation. A lot of these names, particularly in the west of the county, are associated with settlements which survived through to the medieval period or today, as has been shown in the Sweetworthy example. Elsewhere, however, such names are only associated with empty fields. This has led both Michael Costen and Nicholas Corcos in particular to argue that such names could indicate that a substantial change in the pattern of settlement occurred in certain parts of Somerset in the late Saxon and early medieval periods.[19] Such a dramatic shift in settlement pattern would be understandable in terms of the general model of village origins and nucleation that has been postulated already for other parts of the country (see above).

I have argued elsewhere that the extinction of free status and the 'manorialisation' or 'feudalisation' of estates in the period 1066 to 1086 may

Development of medieval rural settlement in Somerset

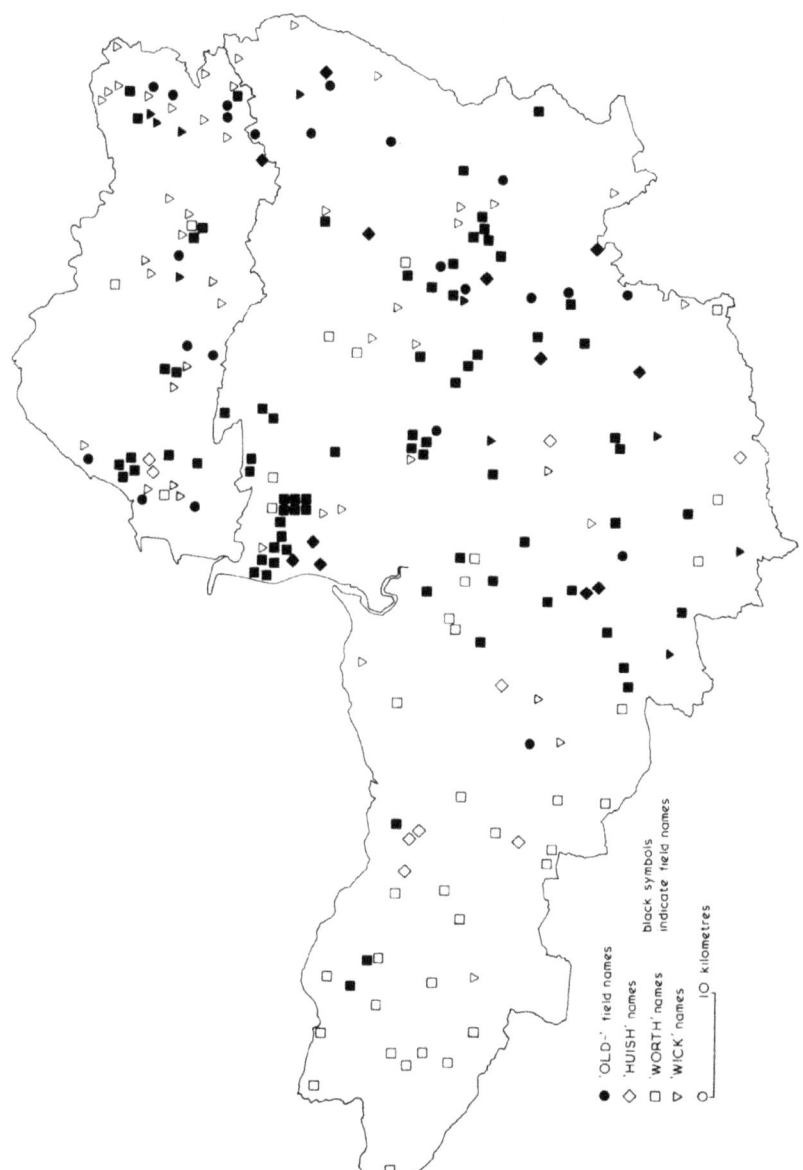

Fig. 4 Somerset—the distribution of certain place-name elements

also have resulted in the creation of nucleated settlements and the abandonment of an existing dispersed pattern. Other, rather less fruitful lines of enquiry have included an examination of the incidence of 'solskifte' in the county and of whether the existence of apparently planned field systems can be equated with planned villages. The investigation of early references to 'waste', together with destruction of settlements in the civil wars of the mid-twelfth century, as possible opportunities for the replanning of settlements has also been considered.[20] On balance it would seem that an approach based on the ownership and tenantry of individual estates in the eleventh and twelfth centuries may well prove most fruitful in further elucidating the circumstances in which certain settlement and field system changes took place.

If these lines of enquiry prove to be useful in developing our hypotheses about settlement origins and change in the county, then there will remain the major problem of explaining the incidence and extent of colonisation in the late Saxon and medieval periods. With the suggestion above of a widespread pattern of small settlements all across the landscape of Somerset by the later Saxon period there exists much less likelihood of extensive tracts of under-used land available for colonisation, as well as a lot less opportunity for groups of farmers to create new settlements in the centuries following the Norman conquest.

This is not to say that there was settlement everywhere in the pre-Norman period; it is unlikely that the highest parts of Exmoor, the Quantocks and the Brendons were settled—there is no evidence of abandoned farmsteads on the flat plateau tops—although at very high levels around the edge there were certainly settlements in existence by Domesday Book (1086), as is witnessed by the example of Bagley. Similarly, the Levels were not settled on the lower, seasonally waterlogged parts especially in the peat fen areas. Nevertheless, all of the small mounds and islands in the Levels seem to have been settled by the late Saxon period—some with agricultural communities such as Bradney, Peasy and Crook in Bawdrip parish or Horsey in Bridgwater parish, others with small monastic communities or groups of hermits as at Nyland in Cheddar (Andredesey), Marchey in Wookey (Martinsey), Godney near Glastonbury, Aller where the Danish king Guthrum was baptized, or the enigmatic site at Oath nearby where there was a medieval hermitage of unknown origin. Even if these upland and lowland areas were not fully settled, and indeed are still not, they were clearly well used as part of the overall agricultural system.

The same argument can be used for the extensive areas of woodland in existence in the county in the eleventh century.[21] Traditionally archaeologists, and even more so geographers, have seen woodland both as something 'left over' after all the other land uses, especially arable, have been accounted for, and as useless areas waiting to be developed by colonisation involving clearance of trees (assarting) and the building of new settlements. Apart from the fact that woodland is of very great economic importance to pre-industrial societies as the main source of timber for building and of wood for fuel, fencing and a host of minor uses, it is easily overlooked that these activities in the woods, together with any use of such areas for pasturage or hunting, would have necessitated many people living in or near woodlands.[22] Far from being empty tracts of little used land, woodland constituted an important and complementary part of the medieval economy supplying commodities that were not readily available in the open, more intensively settled and arable producing parts of the countryside.

Of course clearance of woodland took place and, as in most parts of England, there are frequent documentary references in Somerset to assarts being created and the breaking in of new land. This occurred particularly in the wooded Forest of Selwood, on the east side of the county extending into Wiltshire, and the areas around the Forest of Neroche in the south-west of Somerset.[23] But there are no references to the creation of large numbers of new settlements and nothing in the documents suggests that this was taking place.

Some accounts indeed imply the opposite, suggesting that the woodlands had a substantial population living and farming within them. With the creation of the Carthusian monastery of Witham, for example, in the late twelfth century, 150 people had to be resettled and compensation arranged for the destruction of their buildings and fields.[24] Yet this monastery was founded in the Forest of Selwood in what has traditionally been seen as impenetrable, undeveloped wildwood. Colonisation of such areas (perhaps re-colonisation would be a more useful concept, since in many cases there had clearly been either prehistoric or Romano-British occupation) must have taken place long before the first documentary references become available, perhaps in the seventh or eighth centuries. What we are seeing in the references of the twelfth and thirteenth centuries is predominantly a change of economy from wood-pasture use to increased arable: unlike the previous land use this necessitated the clearance of trees.

On the Levels a similar picture can be built up, particularly on the coastal clay belt from Hinkley Point to Avonmouth. As Michael Williams has shown, the drainage of this area is not referred to in the documents of the great estates from the twelfth century onwards and hence is likely to have taken place earlier, presumably accompanied by an expansion of settlement onto these flatlands.[25] The research of both Roger Leech, looking at the Parrett basin in the Roman period, and of Sam Nash, examining buried deposits in the Burnham on Sea area, suggests that much of the contemporary Romano-British landscape is now buried beneath up to at least a metre of marine clay.[26] Any colonisation of the clay belt is thus likely to have taken place in the centuries between the fifth and the twelfth, with perhaps the late Saxon period being the most likely.

All of this evidence makes it very difficult to argue for extensive colonisation in the medieval period together with the creation of new settlements. It will be important in future to isolate the new part of the settlement pattern for the Saxon and medieval periods, if it can be shown to exist. It will be interesting to see if the archaeology of any sites excavated can be shown to display aspects of colonisation in this period.

Two isolated deserted farms in the north of the county demonstrate the problems of definition clearly. At Pickwick in Dundry parish excavation showed that the site had been occupied in prehistoric (Iron Age) and Romano-British as well as medieval times; the site was only abandoned in the nineteenth century with a move to a new model farm situated on flatter land below Dundry Hill.[27] Given the difficulties of interpreting the structural evidence and the almost total lack of pottery from the sixth to eleventh centuries in Somerset, can we really assume that this site was abandoned in the post-Roman and Saxon periods to be resettled again in the early Middle Ages? Or, as seems more likely to this writer, was the site continuously occupied from prehistoric to modern times? Such a question is critical if the impact of medieval colonisation is to be accurately assessed. For the nearby unexcavated site of Ramspits in Westbury sub Mendip parish, for example, it means two equally valid models for its origin. Either it can be seen as a continuously occupied site—a hamlet left over from the previous era of dispersed settlement in an area of predominantly nucleated villages, or as a colonising farmstead created in the early Middle Ages, beyond the common fields of its mother village, on the upper slopes of the Mendips. It would then represent some final burst of pre-Black Death land hunger by desperate peasants anxious to farm as much of the upper slopes as possible. More sophisticated excavation techniques and far greater rigour in our theoretical approach to such problems are needed to answer such questions.

Later Medieval Settlement Patterns

Putting together the evidence from both eastern and western Somerset it is possible to suggest a model for the development of different settlement patterns in the Saxon and Medieval periods. This includes an assumption of great persistence in land usage and probably in settlement sites from the late prehistoric and Romano-British periods through to the Middle Ages. How far settlement was nucleated in these periods and how much of this survived into the sub- and post-Roman periods we do not know as yet, but in the centuries before *c.* 900 it is likely that the only nucleated settlements of any size were the important royal and ecclesiastical centres as the heads of their respective estates. Such settlements would have housed agricultural officials responsible for running the estates, possibly a high status residence and probably a minster church. These places frequently emerge as the hundredal manors and centres of later times and eventually are developed as simple exchange and later market centres.[28] They are surrounded by lower status agricultural settlements which are dependants of the main 'caputs' and owe labour and other services, and later religious obligations, to it. It must now be presumed that these subsidiary places were smaller, probably farms and hamlets, and primarily agricultural in function. They made up the majority of the places in the Somerset countryside and most were probably in existence by the ninth century.

What then happened to produce the medieval and modern pattern of settlement? Any newer model must now distinguish between the apparently persistent pattern of these dispersed settlements in the west of the county and great changes elsewhere. In many parts of Somerset a degree of nucleation and planning of settlement occurred, probably between the tenth and the twelfth centuries. The reasons were certainly complex but allowance must be made now for greater manorialisation, or feudalisation, resulting in the extinction of what had probably been a freer, more individual and more dispersed pattern of landholding in the pre-Norman period.[29] Also, increased attention to more efficient estate management may have resulted in the agglomeration of certain settlements; this may be hinted at in some of the references in Domesday Book but the process may also have been old even by 1086. Few drastic changes can be distinguished in the abundant documentation surviving from the twelfth century for the extensive Glastonbury Abbey estates, suggesting perhaps that any replanning of estates, villages and fields had already taken place by 1066. The same may be true of royal, episcopal and other ecclesiastical estates.

With so much development apparently completed by the eleventh and twelfth centuries, the tenth century becomes worthy of careful consideration. This is, after all, the period of perhaps greatest strength and influence of the Wessex royal household, the period of Dunstan's monastic reforms and the creation and development of many towns in the county reflecting a developing and diversifying rural economy.[30] What better time to redevelop rural settlements to provide the surplus in commodities needed to fuel the growth and development of such a society?

But the changes could not have taken place everywhere in the county and only in a relatively few places did they result in very large nucleated villages in the middle of their open fields with few other settlements in the vicinity. The processes involved were clearly not as all-consuming as they were further east in the country, although they seem to have been more developed than in the neighbouring county of Devon.

Such a model of settlement origin, growth and development in the post-Roman period in Somerset will clearly demand a great deal of further refining and modification but at least there is now a framework into which new research can be fitted. It is the writer's intention to use the parish of Shapwick in the centre of the county near Glastonbury to test a number of these ideas over the next few years.

The nucleated settlements resulting from the processes described above are very varied in their topography (figs. 5 and 6). Until recently this aspect of

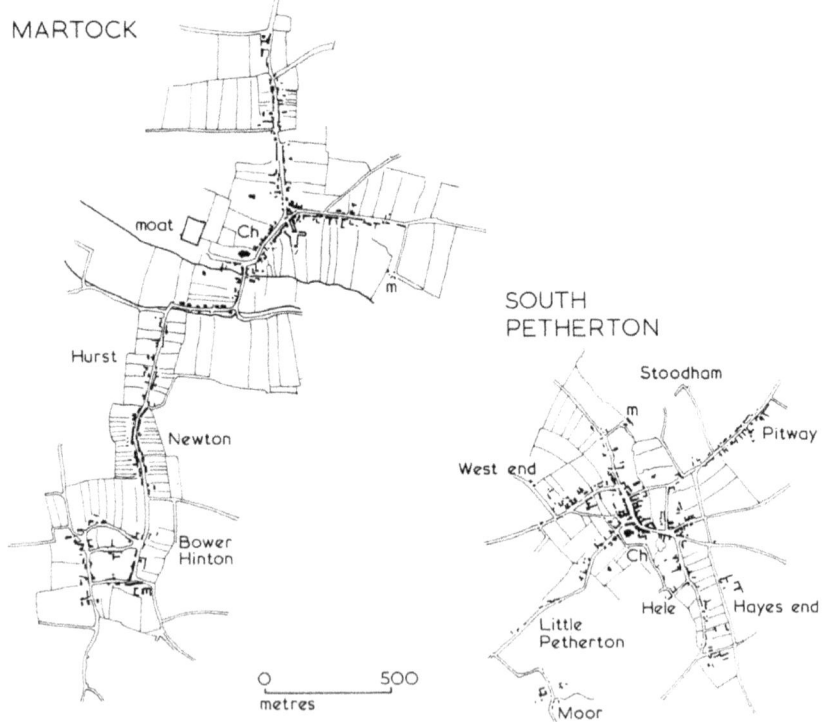

Fig. 5   Composite ('polyfocal') village plans in Somerset

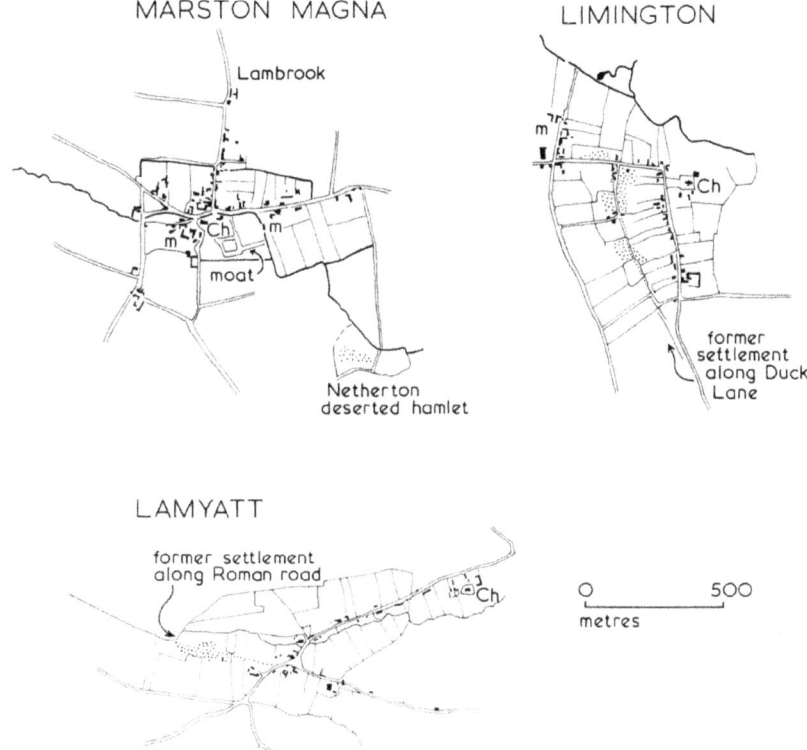

Fig. 6 Selected village plans in Somerset

settlement development had been little studied in Somerset but a preliminary survey of village plans in the county has now been published.[31] While one might argue with this in detail, it does at least show the extent, for example, of the main types of village plan as defined by Brian Roberts. There are relatively few large composite or polyfocal villages in the county—the best examples are Bishops Lydeard, Martock and South Petherton—but a number of the smaller nucleations have complex plans made up of several discrete centres. Lopen, for example, has two main parts reflecting the two manors in the Middle Ages; Limington has three main elements, a church area, manor and mill area and abandoned village street—the present village seems to be along the back lane of the medieval village; Marston Magna has two elements to the plan, the eastern one of which must be the earlier, with consequent implications for the village plan. At Lamyatt there seems to be a rare example of one plan replacing another on a different alignment. In this case an abandoned area of house platforms and boundary banks within an embanked enclosure aligned east-west on the Roman road from the Fosse Way to the temple on Lamyatt Beacon has been replaced by a string of cottages and farms aligned north-east south-west from the medieval church to a small green and running through the earlier alignment.[32]

It is difficult to assess the full extent of planned settlements in the county, particularly as it is not certain in every case that some degree of regularity of plan necessarily implies rigid planning of village outline and properties. In some cases, however, such as with Woolavington, Edington, Cossington, Shapwick, Ashcott and Walton, villages on the Glastonbury Abbey estate to the north of the Polden ridge in the middle of the county, it is difficult to see how such regularity could have arisen without deliberate planning unless the patterns of village roads and properties are following pre-existing patterns of land and road boundaries. At Shapwick (fig. 7), however, even a preliminary analysis of the village plan, as shown on no less than four eighteenth-century maps, shows how the regular pattern of roads and properties partly disrupts and partly fits in with the pre-existing road network.[33]

By the early fourteenth century the extent and intensity of medieval settlement was at its peak and it is now well known that a substantial part of this pattern disappeared in the succeeding centuries.[34] The reasons for the decline of settlements and the incidence of the desertion of villages have been well studied but relatively little detailed work has been done for Somerset. What is clear is that there are no catastrophic reasons for deserted villages in the county; there are, for example, no definite cases of landlords evicting peasants from their holdings in the ways referred to in the documentation for the midlands. Nor were most of the deserted sites formerly large villages. Indeed, most of them in Somerset were no more than hamlets of more important, and usually still extant, places elsewhere. The abandoned villages where churches as well as peasant houses have been demolished, indicating that the places were probably fully developed villages, include Rowley alias Wittenham in Farleigh Hungerford, Fairoak in Berkley, Woodwick in Freshford, West Dowlish in Dowlish Wake, and Goose Bradon and Earnshill in Curry Rivel. The latter place also provides an example of a probable Black Death desertion, since its church was combined with that of Curry Rivel in the 1350s because there were no people left on account of the *pestilenciam*. Elsewhere, as for example at Witcombe in Martock, the plague clearly did great damage but sites were eventually resettled—there is still a hamlet at Witcombe.[35]

Development of medieval rural settlement in Somerset

Fig. 7 Shapwick—changes in the village plan between 1764 and 1885

What the Black Death and subsequent plagues did do was to weaken the village community and the communal way in which many medieval field systems were operated. Far from evicting tenants, it looks as if landlords tried to maintain their farming activities and rents much as before but with gradually failing effect. A good example occurs at Speckington, a hamlet of Yeovilton, where the lord let three sixty-acre farms at a low rent 'until better tenants do come'.[36] For the peasants who remained there were ample opportunities to better themselves. Unlike many parts of the country there were alternatives to arable farming in the South West. As elsewhere, sheep farming increased in importance, although this could never be a great employer; cattle raising on the Levels together with milk and particularly cheese production, however, may well have increased at this time. But of greatest importance was the existence of the west of England cloth industry, a later medieval development making Somerset, along with Wiltshire and Gloucestershire, a major industrial region from the fifteenth century onwards.[37]

The wealth created by this industry is well represented in the county in the numerous small late-medieval manor houses of the gentry families and in the enormous numbers of fine late-medieval church buildings, particularly towers, to be seen all over the region (Fig. 8). Clearly the situation was not all one of 'crisis and decline'.[38] Many villages gradually decayed, although where we can see the evidence from documents it is a slow protracted process; at Bineham, for example, detailed documentary research by Robert Dunning failed to find a final date for the abandonment of the hamlet in Long Sutton parish, although there was only one house occupied in the seventeenth century.[39] At Mudford rationalisation of the fields of the lord's holding and redistribution to the tenant farmers was going on in the sixteenth century in an attempt to provide increased sustenance for the farmers' families, but still the majority of the hamlets in the parish declined drastically.[40] The small manor houses at Lytes Cary, Coker Court, Cothay, Tickenham Court, Martock and Hutton, together with the two fine late fourteenth-century castles in the county at Nunney and Farleigh Hungerford, all show the secular wealth of some of the gentry families of the time, while the number of late-medieval church buildings demonstrates the investment of the population in matters more religious.[41]

Conclusion

The origin, development, partial decline and change of the patterns and forms of settlement in medieval Somerset can be viewed as a complex set of dynamic processes. No single reason can be suggested for the origin of the county's

Fig 8. Batcombe church tower: a will of 1540 refers to its construction

settlements, no single line of development postulated and no obvious catastrophic reason given for the demise of any particular place. However uncertain we are of the evidence, it is becoming clear that great complexity lies behind the changes we see in these ancient settlements in the landscape. Since the recognition of the phenomenon of deserted medieval villages in the late 1940s, research into medieval rural settlements has quickened and widened in scope to include not only the abandoned parts of the pattern but also the growth and development of the less nucleated elements. In Somerset research did not get under way until the 1970s, but, as has been shown in this article it is already possible to suggest from recent work some of the major lines of development in the county's post-Roman settlement history.

In future at least two lines of enquiry will be necessary. Firstly, it is essential that some of the suggestions made here are followed up. For example, among many possibilities it will be necessary to look at the ownership of settlements at particular dates to see if similar developments reflect likely estate policies of certain owners. Consistently used measurements will need to be looked for, together with much more fieldwork to locate the relict parts of earlier village and hamlet plans. It will be necessary eventually to excavate, at least in part, certain areas of some settlements. Detailed documentary, topographical and cartographic research on a few settlements rich in both historical records and early maps, as well as in earthworks, early buildings and field features will be essential: Shapwick may well provide an example of this.

Secondly, and rather more importantly, it will be necessary to develop a sound theoretical basis for our examination and eventual explanation of the changes we observe in Somerset's settlements over a millenium. Because the changes are complex and the reasons behind them not likely to be open to simple analysis it is essential that a systems approach is adopted.[42] Only if we attempt to explain the interactions between changes in medieval society, the economy, population dynamics, developments in technology and so on are we ever likely to begin to understand what we see when we go out into the Somerset countryside.

Notes

1. M. Aston, 'The medieval pattern AD 1000-1500' in M. Aston and I. Burrow (eds.), *The Archaeology of Somerset* (1982), 122-33; M. Aston, 'Rural settlement in Somerset: some preliminary thoughts' in D. Hooke (ed.), *Medieval Villages: a Review of Current Work* (1985), 81-100; M. Aston, 'Post-Roman central places in Somerset' in E. Grant (ed.), *Central Places, Archaeology and History* (1986), 47-77; M. Aston, 'Settlement patterns and forms' in M. Aston (ed.), *Aspects of the Medieval Landscape of Somerset* (1988), 67-81.

2. For general accounts of the prehistoric, Roman and post-Roman periods in the county see M. Aston and I. Burrow (eds.), *The Archaeology of Somerset* (note 1). For more detailed accounts see B. and J. Coles, *Sweet Track to Glastonbury* (1986); R.H. Leech, 'Romano-British Rural Settlement in South Somerset and North Dorset' unpublished Ph.D. thesis (1977), I. Burrow, *Hillfort and Hill-top Settlement in Somerset in the First Millennium AD* (BAR 91, 1981), P.A. Rahtz, 'The Dark Ages 400-700 AD' in Aston and Burrow (eds.), (note 1), P.A. Rahtz and P.J. Fowler, 'Somerset AD 400-700' in P.J. Fowler (ed.), *Archaeology and the Landscape* (1972), 187-221.
3. C. Taylor, *Village and Farmstead* (1983); J. Chapelot and R. Fossier, *The Village and House in the Middle Ages* (1985); D. Hooke (ed.), *Medieval Villages* (note 1).
4. *Somerset Levels Papers 1-14* (1975-88); I. Simmons and M. Tooley (eds), *The Environment in British Prehistory* (1981).
5. G. Jones, 'Multiple Estates and Early Settlement' in P. Sawyer (ed.), *English Medieval Settlement* (1979), 9-34; M. Aston, 'Post-Roman Central Places in Somerset' (note 1); J. Blair (ed.), *Minsters and Parish Churches: the Local Church in Transition 950-1200* (1988).
6. P. Rahtz, *The Saxon and Medieval Palaces at Cheddar: Excavations 1960-2* (BAR 65, 1979).
7. M. Aston, 'Deserted farmsteads on Exmoor and the Lay Subsidy of 1327 in west Somerset', *Proc. Som. Arch. Nat. Hist. Soc.*, 127 (1983), 71-104.
8. H.S.A. Fox, 'Contraction: desertion and dwindling of dispersed settlement in a Devon parish', *Annual Report of the Medieval Village Research Group*, 31 (1983), 40-2.
9. F. H. Dickinson, 'Kirby's Quest for Somerset', *Somerset Record Society*, 3 (1889).
10. Documents for Brompton Regis include estate maps (1804) and records (1801) of Lord Egremont's estates (S.R.O., DD/WY), the 'Names of Estates' in the tithe award (S.R.O., D/D/Rt 1841) and the 1629 'note taken by Henry Nicolls vicar, of every man and woman seats in ye church' (SRO, D/P/b re 7/3/1).
11. S. Everett, 'The Domesday geography of three Exmoor parishes', *Proc. Som. Arch. Nat. Hist. Soc.*, 112 (1968), 54-60; C. and F. Thorn (eds.), *Domesday Book, 8, Somerset* (1980).
12. F.W. Weaver, 'Barlinch Priory', *Proc. Som. Arch. Nat. Hist. Soc.*, 54 (1908), 79-106.
13. R. Bush, R.W. Dunning and M. Siraut in R.W. Dunning (ed.), *Victoria County History of Somerset*, vol. 5 (1985).
14. See air photograph and discussion in Aston (1983) (note 7).
15. P. Leach, 'A Deserted farm in the Brendon Hills (Hurscombe)', *Proc. Som. Arch. Nat. Hist. Soc.*, 126 (1982), 43-60.
16. For deserted medieval villages in Somerset, see M. Aston in Aston and Burrow (eds.) (1982), M. Aston (Note 1) and references in the Medieval Village Research Group annual reports.
17. See especially G. Foard, 'Systematic fieldwalking and the investigation of Saxon settlement in Northamptonshire', *World Archaeology*, 9 (1978), 357-374, and C. Taylor, *Village and Farmstead* (note 3).
18. M. Costen, 'Huish and Worth: Old English survivals in a later landscape', in D.

Brown, J. Campbell and S.C. Hawkes (eds.), *Anglo-Saxon Studies in Archaeology and History* (forthcoming).
19. M. Costen, 'Rimpton in Somerset', *Southern History*, 7 (1985), 13-24; N. Corcos, 'Early estates on the Poldens and the origin of settlement at Shapwick', *Proc. Som. Arch. Nat. Hist. Soc.*, 127 (1983), 47-53.
20. M. Aston in note 1; M. Aston, 'Settlement Patterns and Forms' (note 1), based on ideas in P. Allerston, 'English village development: findings from the Pickering district of North Yorkshire', *Trans. Inst. Brit. Geographers*, 51 (1970), 95-109 where the use of 'old' as a field name is suggested as significant (and see Fig. 3 here); J. Sheppard, 'Medieval village planning in Northern England: Some evidence from Yorkshire', *J. Hist. Geog.*, 2 (1976), 3-20.
21. O. Rackham, 'Woods, Hedges and Forests' in M. Aston (1988), 13-31 (note 1).
22. O. Rackham, *Trees and Woodland in the British Landscape* (1976); O. Rackham, *Ancient Woodland: its History, Vegetation and Uses in England* (1980).
23. See M. Aston (1988), 'Land use and field systems' (note 1).
24. D.H. Farmer, *St. Hugh of Lincoln* (1985).
25. M. Williams, *The Draining of the Somerset Levels* (1970).
26. R. Leech, 'The Somerset Levels in the Romano-British period' in T. Rowley (ed.), *The Evolution of Marshland Landscapes* (1981), 20-51; S.G. Nash, 'A deep water inlet at Highbridge, a precis of a paper' *Proc. Som. Arch. Nat. Hist. Soc.*, 117 (1973), 97-101.
27. K. Barton, 'Pickwick Farm, Dundry, Somerset', *Proc. University of Bristol Spelaeological Society*, 12(1) (1969), 99-112.
28. M. Aston, in Grant (ed.) (note 1).
29. M. Aston, in Hooke (ed.) (note 1).
30. M. Aston, 'The towns of Somerset' in J. Haslam (ed.), *Anglo-Saxon Towns in Southern England* (1984), 167-201.
31. B. Roberts, *The Making of the English Village* (1987).
32. For Lopen, see Aston in Hooke (ed.) (note 1); for Limington and Lamyatt, see Aston 1988 (note 1).
33. For Shapwick, see Aston 1988 (note 1).
34. M.W. Beresford, *The Lost Villages of England* (1954); M. W. Beresford and J.G. Hurst (eds), *Deserted Medieval Villages* (1971); C. Dyer, 'Deserted medieval villages in the West Midlands', *Econ. Hist. Rev.*, 2nd ser., 25 (1982), 19-34.
35. M. Aston 1988 (note 1).
36. R.W. Dunning (ed.), *Victoria County History of Somerset* vol. 3(1974), 171.
37. J.H. Bettey, *Wessex from AD 1000* (1986).
38. M. Havinden, *The Somerset Landscape* (1981).
39. For Bineham, see R.W. Dunning, 'Long Sutton' in R.W. Dunning (ed.), 154 (note 36).
40. M. Aston, 'Deserted settlements in Mudford parish, Yeovil', *Proc. Som. Arch. Nat. Hist. Soc.*, 121 (1977), 41-53.
41. J. Harvey, *The Perpendicular Style 1330-1485* (1978).
42. C. Renfrew, *Approaches to Social Archaeology* (1984), esp. chaps. 9, 10.

Peasant farmers, patterns of settlement and *pays*: transformations in the landscapes of Devon and Cornwall during the later Middle Ages

by Harold Fox

This paper is based upon work carried out over the past few years for the volume of *The Agrarian History of England and Wales (1349–1500)* covering the later Middle Ages.[1] The materials for the study of agrarian history in the South West during this period are neither exceptionally numerous nor exceptional in their detail. The historian has to cross and re-cross the same documentary series in search of facts and figures to illustrate different themes, to pursue arguments from manor to manor, from one type of document to another, link by link along the frail chain of evidence. There is a danger that he may become obsessed with the sources, his models, the period itself. As a research student I was told that to claim that a chosen period is more important than any other marks the beginnings of mild academic eccentricity; but nevertheless I shall try here to show that in terms of the development of landscape, countrymen in Devon and Cornwall during the later Middle Ages took part in transformations of prime importance, giving us much that we see about us in the countryside today.

Embedded in as influential a work as Postan's chapter on England for the *Cambridge Economic History of Europe* is the statement that 'most of Devonshire's coombes and valleys and much of Cornwall's interior were not fully occupied until the thirteenth century.' The source of that view is not hard to find: in W.G.Hoskins's magisterial essay on 'The making of the agrarian landscape' of Devon, published in 1952, and in W.G.V. Balchin's *Cornwall*, part of a series edited by Hoskins.[2] Behind their remarks, no doubt, lay the influence of the chronological model of Marc Bloch who had called the twelfth and thirteenth centuries *l'âge des grands défrichements*, a model which we are only now becoming brave enough to realize is by no means appropriate to the majority of English landscapes.³ It was then believed (although Hoskins later radically revised his views on this point) that post-Roman Devon was 'sparsely settled' and that 'no considerable native population remained to complicate the life of the new [West Saxon] settlers' in the seventh century.⁴ From that conviction naturally followed the view that it took many centuries of reclamation, of the establishment of new farms, of the penetration of remote coombes, until the landscape assumed that relatively full appearance which it has when viewed through the evidence of place-names first recorded in the thirteenth and early fourteenth centuries—movements which supposedly gathered momentum exponentially until they reached their peak in a period of very rapidly expanding population in the two and a half centuries following the Norman conquest.

The logic of these arguments has been shattered by recent research on post-Roman Dumnonia, by Herbert Finberg, Charles Thomas, Susan Pearce, Oliver Padel and Lynette Olson in particular.⁵ Their work and my own faltering researches on this period lead to the conclusion that a good deal of the basic bone structure of the countryside—some settlement sites and ecclesiastical sites, some estates and boundaries—was already in place in the post-Roman period; to understand the landscapes of the South West we shall have in the future to do our best to recreate more of those early Dumnonian outlines.⁶ The second formative phase, in my view, took place in the later Middle Ages, during a period of declining population, when in many respects the details, the *minutiae*, of agrarian landscapes in the South West began to assume the shapes and forms with which we are familiar today. Here I shall first examine some of the experiences of rural populations in this period—in the conviction that there can be no landscape history as a respectable subject unless we write as much about people as about the cultural landscapes which they created—before looking at changes in the patterns of farms, fields and farming regions where they lived and worked.

Peasant Farmers in the Landscape

Many standard accounts of the Black Death state that it reached England through the Dorset port of Melcombe Regis around the Feast of St. John the Baptist (24 June) 1348. But before this, on 16 June, the sheriff of Devon failed to appear before the Exchequer because of illness, and none of his staff could take his place because all had died of plague. The disease reached Cornwall early in 1349, several months before it affected the Midlands and the North.⁷ Neither the peninsular shape of Devon and Cornwall, nor a dispersed settlement pattern, served to lessen the impact of plague, as an earlier generation of historians supposed.⁸ When William of Worcester visited

Bodmin he was shown a register in the priory there which claimed that 1500 people had died in the years immediately following 1348; the inhabitants of Truro and Helston complained of their towns as 'depleted' and 'uninhabitable'. As well as this evidence from small country towns, a decline in tin production and in fishing activity, and deaths among the landless, all show that plague left no sorts or conditions of men untouched.[9] The province was relatively highly commercialized in the fourteenth century, which made for constant movements of people engaged in buying and selling and in seasonal employment in the stannaries; movements of men with their livestock may also have helped to spread disease, particularly if—as now claimed by one writer—mortality in 1348-9 was the result not only of bubonic plague but also of diseases prevalent in domesticated animals.[10]

We should not blame bubonic plague—the outbreaks of 1348-9, 1361, 1369 and others—for the total extent of population decline in later medieval Devon and Cornwall. It has been argued that population levels were beginning to fall before 1348, through self-regulatory mechanisms in a society whose economy had expanded too fast and too far. In the early fourteenth century we hear of land lying abandoned, particularly on the infertile hill-slopes of East Devon, and in the moory landscapes beyond Truro in far western Cornwall where successive reeves of Helston in Kirrier were all committed to Launceston gaol in the 1340s for their failure to collect expected levels of rent from a farming population which was experiencing difficulties on marginal lands.[11] We hear of destitution in a countryside where smallholders predominated: of the twenty-six tenants of Ottery St. Mary who, in 1334, abandoned their holdings because they could not pay the royal tenth; of those three poor itinerant women 'of Devonshire' who were fined for gleaning on the Somerset manor of Shapwick (they were 'pardoned because dead').[12] Then again, it is probable that not all of the years of heavy mortalities during the fifteenth century were years of bubonic plague, for historians now diagnose other serious maladies in that sickly century.[13] Finally, growth in the practice of keeping servants in husbandry—a practice later to be widespread in the South West—may have contributed to the fall in population through delaying age at marriage.[14] Precisely how great that fall was we shall never know. At a national scale it might have been by as much as fifty or fifty-five per cent between the beginning of the fourteenth century and the beginning of the sixteenth, to give that 'very thinly inhabited' countryside from 'the borders of Scotland ... to Bristol and into Cornwall' which a Venetian visitor and his informants marvelled at in the 1490s.[15]

One important transformation which took place among the farming population of the South West, with profound effects upon the landscape, was the decline of the smallholder. The extent to which the expansive tendencies of the early Middle Ages had reduced the sizes of holdings is clear from many sources. For example, the great survey made for Edward Woodstock when created Duke of Cornwall in 1337 reveals that Helstone, on the manor of that name in Trigg Hundred, consisted of twelve smallholders with a mean farm size of thirteen acres, by no means on prime agricultural land; at Tregoodwell four peasant farmers held eighteen acres each and four nine acres; and so on throughout the manor, with the exception of freeholds and moory holdings out towards Rough Tor which were larger. At Dunnabridge on rocky Dartmoor soil at a thousand feet a new hamlet was established, so the record tells us, in about 1300, eloquent testimony to the largely marginal nature of early medieval settlement expansion; each of the new farms was of nineteen and a fifth acres, smallholdings indeed given the nature of the site. The same can be said of the new early medieval settlement at Brown Willy high on Bodmin Moor where four smallholders initially shared about twenty acres of infield.[16] Even smaller holdings are recorded in some other parts of early medieval England,[17] but these examples are nevertheless impressive evidence of the extent to which, even on some of the poorest soils of the South West, pressure of population before the Black Death led to the creation of a countryside of smallholders.

Changes in farm sizes were not suddenly apparent after 1348 for the simple reason that, following the epidemic, formerly landless men stepped into vacant holdings: accounts of Dartmoor tell us as much, explaining that payments formerly made by the *censarii* or landless declined in 1349 'because they take land and are quit of their *censar*'.[18] But slowly, as population fell to lower levels the documents begin to reveal vacant holdings which were not immediately taken up by tenants. Court rolls from Sidbury, for example, record an increase in the size of the pool of vacancies in the 1430s and again in the 1460s; those of Stoke Fleming show a substantial pool in the middle decades of the fifteenth century. Assession rolls of the Duchy of Cornwall likewise contain lists of lands *in manu domini*.[19] Under such circumstances, with vacant holdings readily available, it was easy for the resourceful—and lucky—tenant to promote himself higher up the ladder of landholding. John Fowlesdon of Sidbury surrenders a cottage and simultaneously takes up a holding clearly of some size, for the fine was 40s. Cottagers of Stokenham manor who promoted themselves to become occupiers of full holdings are revealed by the family names of Chaunte and Viel (among others), borne only by cottagers in a rental of *c.* 1347 but by occupiers of full farm holdings about thirty years later.[20] If cottagers were able to break into the ranks of holders of more than a few acres, accumulation of holdings must have been even easier for tenants already in possession of some farmland.[21] On five manors for which it is possible to calculate farm sizes both before 1348 and towards the end of the later Middle Ages, the mean acreage of holdings rose from twenty-two to forty-seven acres. At some of these places the total rental declined by only a little but behind the facade of totals there could take place profound changes in the size of the farming population and the sizes of farms.[22]

Another important and related transformation was the decline in hereditary tenure: farmers were no longer as attached as they had perforce once been to particular holdings but, with so much land easily available, could move away from the old patrimony.[23] In a rental of Newton St. Cyres made in 1408 the occupiers of four of the conventionary holdings bore the same name as the 'former' *(nuper)* occupier—two of these cases were examples of succession by widows—but on the remaining twenty a change in family name had occurred.[24] Again, the 'wandering' of holdings between families is well illustrated by a fifteen-acre farm at Fentonadle which passed from Warin Dirman, to Richard Harry, to Christopher Fentenaswell, to John Berman in the space of twenty-four years between 1347 and 1371.[25] Rapid circulation of holdings among families in the South West may be explained in part by circumstances which brought hereditary succession to a low ebb in most parts of later medieval England: high mortality, particularly among the young, and greater availability of land. In the South West in particular, the many opportunities for sons to accumulate capital in non-agricultural occupations and then to acquire their own holdings were no doubt important.[26] Moreover, on many Cornish estates, and on some in Devon, large numbers of occupiers were *conventionarii* holding under a system of regularly re-negotiated leases which meant that all tenants simultaneously surrendered their holdings every seven years, each to be bargained for anew.[27] The presence of these tenures on one manor must have stimulated the land market of its whole neighbourhood, giving additional momentum to inter-manorial migration in search of a first, or a better, farm. Such movements must have been very common to judge from turnover rates in names of tenants. For example, on the manor of Stokenham only 25 per cent of the names of farming families recorded in a rental of *c.* 1347 were still present in *c.* 1360; by 1548 only 11 per cent of the pre-plague names remained.[28] The precise validity of such figures (and of some others given in this paragraph) depends of course on the degree to which surnames were hereditary; they may, therefore, slightly over-estimate the circulation of farming families between manors under conditions of a 'relaxed' land market during the later Middle Ages.[29] It would be fascinating to know more about the ultimate 'horizons' of such movements—were they confined to specific localities?—and work in progress on the volume for Devon in the University of Leicester's *English Surnames Survey* may yet give us the answers.[30] We need also to know more about how movement between farm and farm came to be 'stabilized' towards the end of the fifteenth century: there are indications then of more reluctance to move and a growing desire to secure an inheritance by naming heirs in leases, developments presumably associated with the beginnings of growth in population which gradually brought with it a scarcity of available farm holdings.[31] Surely relevant in this context is the fact that it is from the end of the fifteenth century that many substantial and enduring medieval farmhouses have survived, in Devon at least.[32] A situation in which farms frequently changed hands was not conducive to much serious attention to the farmhouse, whereas more stable conditions led to investment and rebuilding. It is a moot point as to whether or not such secure farmsteads and their large, enclosed farmlands still justify the epithet 'peasant' used in the title of this section.[33]

There were important changes, too, in patterns of labouring life. The number of labourers dwindled. From the thirteenth and early fourteenth centuries there are many references to cottagers who held their cottages partly in return for work on the demesne or who had gained a precarious toehold on the land by reclaiming an acre or two of waste which must have provided some livelihood to supplement a labouring wage. In the former category were the twenty-eight cottagers at Yealmpton who reaped on the demesne for one day a week in autumn; in the latter were men such as John Ponta and William de Halewille who each held minute acreages of *landiok* (i.e. assart) on the manor of Stoke Climsland. As we have seen, greater availability of land after 1348 opened up new opportunities for promotion of cottagers into the ranks of full landholders. Everywhere their numbers declined accordingly, and at a rate greater than that of occupiers of full holdings, so that by the end of the fourteenth century sources are redolent with references to empty and decayed cottages. Thus at Fremington there were in 1326 as many as thirty-nine cottagers, but 'diverse destroyed cottages' by 1388; seven cottages at Lanherne in 1343 had all disappeared by the fifteenth century; an account for Holcombe Rogus in 1405-6 records a cavernous decayed cottage, presumably once occupied by one Prout and graphically called 'Prothole'.[34] These trends meant that surviving cottagers, because of the scarcity of their labour, could command higher wages: ploughboys working on Tavistock Abbey demesnes earned 3½d. per week in 1334, but 8d. per week by 1414, and wages of labourers working in and about the castles and deer parks of the Duchy of Cornwall rose at once after the Black Death and then doubled between 1380 and 1430.[35]

For some labourers, moreover, the whole pattern of accommodation was transformed by the institution of service in husbandry on a 'live-in' basis.[36]

There were several forces at work to encourage its greater adoption by farmers during the later Middle Ages: high wage levels, for example, and the growing emphasis on pastoral farming, for living-in labourers were especially useful at times of crisis over the birth or illness of livestock.[37] The presence of servants in husbandry may be indirectly inferred from the lay subsidy of 1524-5: at Ashwater no cottagers are recorded in a rental of 1523, yet the subsidy a year later lists twenty-nine men assessed at £1, many of whom were almost certainly servants in husbandry living in farmhouses on the manor's large, engrossed pastoral holdings.[38] Growth in another type of provision of accommodation is apparent from two rentals of the coastal manor of Stokenham where, before the Black Death, there were about ninety occupied cotttages, almost all of them (92 per cent) in the hands of independent cottagers living from labouring and, no doubt, from fishing. By c. 1360 only 41 per cent of a reduced number of cottages were occupied by independent cottagers; the rest were rented for nominal sums by husbandmen, particularly those with large multiple holdings, and presumably used for housing labourers.[39] The system, in evidence on other Devonshire manors,[40] may well have been developed as an inducement to attract a scarce commodity and perhaps to extend the institution of 'living in' to married couples.

It could be argued that such arrangements represented an improvement in living standards, for although independence was lost, employment was guaranteed, at least for the term of the contract, and in the case of servants in husbandry so was subsistence. There of course remained many independent cottagers and labourers who migrated to find seasonal employment in various agricultural and industrial tasks. One could speculate that the latter, itinerant and least secure, group was not unimportant during the later Middle Ages, despite the fact that the period has been described as a 'golden age' for labour. Because wages were so high there were incentives for large farmers to employ labour paid by the day in those tasks for which it was appropriate, leading to flows of itinerants in search of seasonal employment like those men (and women?) of Ashwater in pastoral west Devon who in autumn 1436 made their way over twenty-five miles 'towards *lez Southammys*', the most strongly arable part of Devon.[41] Moreover, in the stannaries both a probable decline in the numbers of farmer-miners (for to combine the two occupations was less necessary as more land became available)[42] and the rise of large-scale capitalistic enterprises must have meant that a growing proportion of those who gained the tin were labourers, employed seasonally in many cases, or for even shorter terms.[43] To a degree, then, some polarization may have taken place within the labouring population during the fourteenth and fifteenth centuries.[44]

Patterns of Settlement and Patterns of Fields

Decline in rural populations, amalgamation of holdings, decay of cottages—all of these had profound effects on patterns of settlement to produce those lonely landscapes, with widely spaced isolated farms, which we see today. There are in the South West few, if any, deserted village sites of the type found in the Midlands, but that is not a product of any greater resiliance of the rural population of Devon and Cornwall, as has been suggested on occasion;[45] it is simply a result of the rarity of villages among the settlement forms of the South West. Analysis of thirteen Cornish manors on the estates of the Duchy of Cornwall, the Arundells and the Bishopric of Exeter shows that unfree tenants lived scattered among a total of 223 settlements, many of them hamlets typically containing between two and six messuages, the rest of them isolated farms; there were no true villages.[46] In Devon, a small number of true nucleated villages—often hundredal centres with therefore a strong chance of survival—accompanied the predominantly dispersed settlement pattern: Axminster in East Devon, for example, where medieval deeds allow one partially to reconstruct the location of farmsteads in the village, and which may already have been a nucleated settlement in 755 when Cyneheard, prince of Wessex, was buried there after a bloody conflict around the bed of the king's concubine.[47] Elsewhere in Devon, as in Cornwall, isolated farmsteads and small hamlets were the rule. In both counties, indeed, the dominant settlement form during the early Middle Ages was the hamlet, a type whose importance in the South West has been neglected in earlier studies, including my own.[48] Thus on the great north Devon manor of Hartland in 1301 all customary tenants lived in hamlets (median size of four messuages)—a total of thirty six in all; on the Duchy's manor of Tybesta beside the infant Fal 88 per cent of the unfree tenants in 1337 lived dispersed in hamlets (median size three messuages), the rest in isolated farmsteads.[49]

Many hamlets probably originated through subdivision among kin of already existing single farms during the early Middle Ages, so that when we find John Ferne, Walter Ferne and Robert Ferne (each with fifteen acres) as occupiers of the hamlet of Hendon, we can surmise that their smallholdings, and thus the very form of the hamlet, arose through the splitting up of a single farm. In the same way we can point to Paul de Luscoys, William de Luscoys and Edward de Luscoys as sole occupiers of the hamlet of Luscoys in 1337, each with twelve English acres.[50] That such subdivisions of customary holdings took place in many cases after the Norman Conquest is suggested by the fact that division was rarely applied (for sound practical reasons) to free tenures held for fractions of knights' fees, tenures whose military obligations we assume to have originated after 1066; many freeholds

Peasant farmers, patterns of settlement and pays   49

of this type remained undivided as substantial holdings and isolated farmsteads. Some hamlets, alternatively, originated as group reclamations, as did the Dartmoor settlement of Dunnabridge: an account of 1301-2 mentions 'new rent' from ninety-six acres, paid by five colonists each of whom took nineteen and a fifth acres, clearly a fifth share of the new assart.[51] Whether the sharing was between kin or between colonists, it tended to produce physically tightly-knit little hamlets whose members looked upon the land in some respects as a communal responsibility, collectively paying rent for vacant holdings, or sharing the use of its rough pastures.[52] There is also the possibility—is there not?—that some hamlets have come down to us from far more distant times, the more humble partners in a dual settlement pattern of defended and undefended sites, rath and clachan, free farmsteads and bond hamlets.[53]

Amalgamation and decay of holdings can have profound effects on patterns of this type, for reduction in a manor's occupied farmsteads, let us say by half, will not destroy a nucleated village but can lead to desertion where settlement is dispersed. Previous work has greatly under-estimated the number of 'lost' or severely contracted sites in the South West. Deserted settlements on the high moorlands have been recorded, and there have been some revealing programmes of excavation.[54] Away from the moorlands a few deserted sites have been identified through fieldwork, such as Beere, dug by E.M. Jope in a pioneering excavation; the Cornish sites excavated, for example, by G. Beresford; and other places (not necessarily all cases of medieval desertion) noted in the excellent parochial check-lists published in *Cornish Archaeology*.[55] But so easily destructible were the cob walling materials of many farmhouses, especially perhaps those of smallholders, that they have often left—earth to earth—only the slightest traces in the field. Documents, in fact, provide the best guide to their identification. There are miscellaneous documentary clues, such as references to unwanted, then decaying, then finally unlettable messuages in the 'defect of rents' sections of reeves' accounts. At 'Cornkee', on the bishop's manor of Tregaire, fifteenth-century accounts tell of decayed cottages, an unlettable farm worth only as much as the 'exits' (probably pasture) of its land; by 1539 the place was described simply as 'one parcel of moor'.[56] Personal names derived from place-names at which no settlement now exists provide some evidence for deserted sites, as M. Aston has shown in his impressive West Somerset survey.[57] Examples from the South Hams of Devon are Honeywell in Halwell and Singmore in Abbotskerswell, only a wood and a barn respectively today, yet the homes of Honewilles and Sengmores in the early fourteenth century.[58] But the most comprehensive guides to settlement contraction in the South West, where they survive, are topographically arranged rentals and extents, which list farms settlement by settlement.⁵⁹ An example is the great extent of Hartland made in about 1365, clearly after a lengthy perambulation of the manor by the steward, for settlement sites are named in the same order as they appear on the map today. The assession rolls of the Duchy of Cornwall, analagous to rentals, drawn up every seven or fourteen years and undoubtedly the best series of documents of this type for any part of medieval England, are also arranged settlement by settlement.⁶⁰ It is the same in other parts of England where dispersed farmsteads prevailed.⁶¹

Fig. 9, based on the Hartland extent of c. 1365 and protraying a wrecked landscape, attempts to show three ways in which hamlets declined in size.⁶² The first of these was *total abandonment* of the land which, by 1365, had affected only Youlden (Y on the map). Youlden was one of the least attractive hamlets in the manor: originally perhaps a single farmstead with thirty acres, by the fourteenth century it had become three smallholdings of fifteen, seven and seven acres all on steep slopes. All of its messuages were empty and its land abandoned by 1365. Another hamlet which eventually disappeared through total abandonment and voluntary emigration of its tenants was Hendon (H), likewise with a landholding structure biased towards smallholders, and likewise on high moory ground. By 1365 five of its messuages had decayed. Reeves' accounts from the 1390s show all the holdings in the lord's hands, later to become rough grazing and 'moor' although at least a folk-memory of the hamlet remained into the nineteenth century when the people of Hartland amused themselves with the rhyme:

> Yennon [Hendon] was a market town
> When Lunnon [London] was a fuzzy down.

Another way in which hamlets declined in size was through *internal engrossing* by which one farm achieved dominance, gradually absorbing the land of the rest as, one by one, they became vacant. Brownsham (B) is a good example: once a hamlet of fourteen farms, by 1365 several of these had been added together and only eight remained, to be reduced to three by 1566. Finally, hamlets could decline through the *attachment* of their land to other places, as one particular farmer built up a multiple holding in two settlements. In some cases the settlements concerned were at a distance (as much as three miles) from one another. An inconvenient and improbable arrangement, it might be suggested. The answer is that the home farm would be used for some cultivation and the supervision of young livestock, while more mature beasts were pastured on the attached farmland at a distance, what a later age was to call a 'feeding farm'. An example from the manor of Hartland in 1365 is a holding at Hendon which had been taken by a farmer at Netherton (N) who no doubt used its moory pastures in this way.⁶³

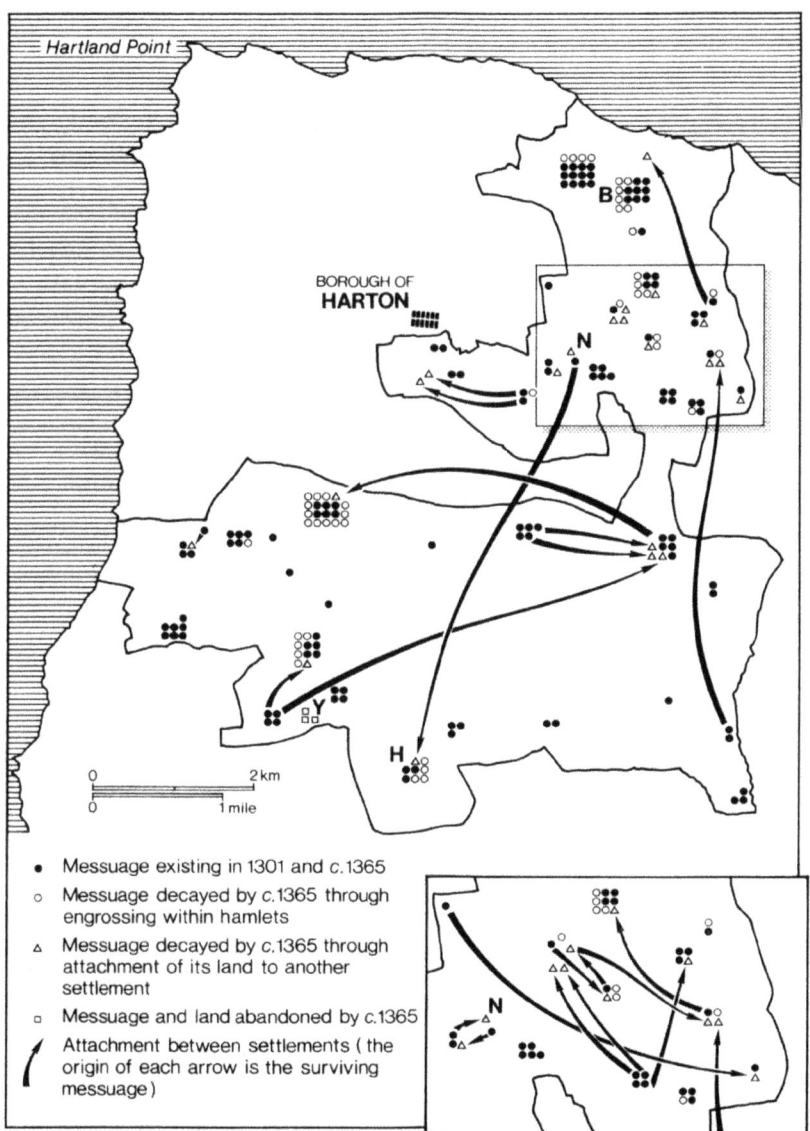

Fig. 9 *Declining settlement patterns on the manor of Hartland, c. 1365. Y, H, B and N are settlements named in the text: Youlden, Hendon, Brownsham and Netherton. Sources: Arundell MSS, rentals and surveys 5, collated with P.R.O., C.133/102/2*

The rental of Hartland in 1365 presents us with a picture of a dispersed settlement pattern about half way through a process of severe contraction. A further decline in the manor's population took place later, leaving thirty-four houses 'vacant' in 1429. By the sixteenth century, altogether eight sites in the manor had become completely deserted, but an even greater number than this had declined in size to become single farmsteads, the characteristic settlement form of the manor today.[64]

In order to examine more closely the end-product of decline in settlement I shall turn to the Duchy's great manor of Helston in Kirrier, which stretched from smiling farmland near the coast in the south to the granite, rock strewn slopes of Carnmenellis, at over 800 feet, in the north.[65] After 1348 farming in the upland sector of the manor was bound to suffer for, as will be shown in the following section, later medieval population decline in Cornwall meant that cultivation could be sustained only on the coastlands, where it was more profitable, and not on the less fertile soils of the moors; difficulties were compounded by declining production of tin in the stannary of Kirrier. The effect on rents and fines was catastrophic: in 1356, the first year after the Black Death when tenants' periodic fines were collected, a large number of holdings were in the lord's hands and on a majority of those which remained tenanted payments were reduced or remitted altogether; in the terminology of the reasons given—*propter debilitatem terre, quia terra morosa*—we can almost see the land reverting back to waste. The Duchy steward, visiting the manor after the pestilence, took the unusual step of writing off many rents in the north, and converting the whole area into a 'chase' whose profits were from sales of 'gorse and heath, the digging of turves and toll on tin'.

Although there was a little recovery of demand for land on Helston manor at the beginning of the fifteenth century, associated with rising production of tin, a further decline in mining activity from the 1430s onwards, lasting for the rest of the fifteenth century, meant that by the end of our period much land was still vacant with many holdings still 'in the chase' and described as 'wasted for many years'.[66] The implications for settlement structure were very great. By the end of the fifteenth century many farms and hamlets lay deserted, particularly relatively new reclamations in the north of the manor. Fig. 10, based on an assession roll of 1486, is in fact a graphic illustration of the way in which, during the later Middle Ages, farms on the coastlands of Cornwall came to be the principal suppliers of grains while those around the moors declined. There was, as at Hartland, much engrossing which led to transformation of hamlets into single farms: thus Carnebone had been three farms in 1337, but by 1486 was held by a single tenant who is described as having 'the whole vill' there. Other settlements became totally deserted, as at adjacent Garlidna, whose land was abandoned, becoming attached as

Peasant farmers, patterns of settlement and pays

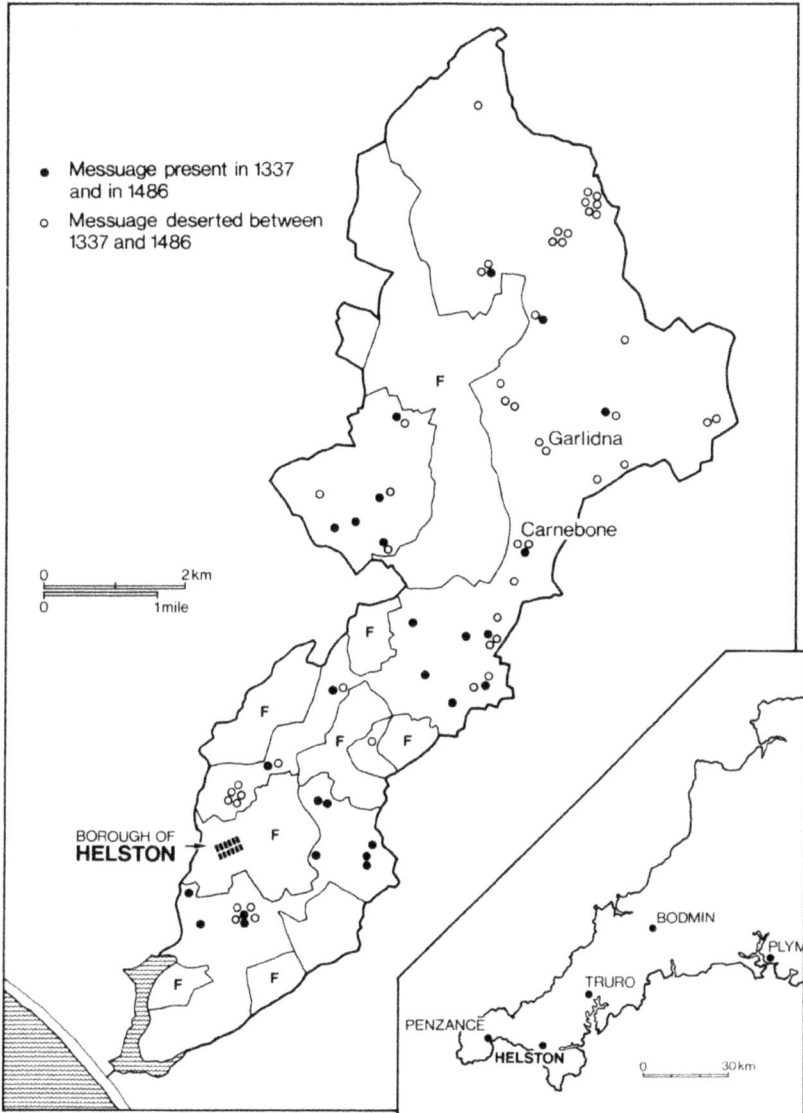

Fig. 10 *Declining settlement patterns on the manor of Helston in Kirrier, 1337–1486. F: the land of free tenements which cannot be accurately mapped at both dates. Sources: P.L. Hull, The Caption of Seisin of the Duchy of Cornwall, 12-24 and P.R.O., E. 306/2/14*

'waste' to Carnebone.[67] The settlement site itself was deserted soon after 1348 and was described as 'tofts' in the later fourteenth century: a toft, as Norden knew well, was 'a little peece of land upon which sometimes was situate a dwelling house'.[68] Of the sites abandoned by 1486 a number were later reoccupied, no doubt with resurgence of mining in later centuries, but of others no trace can be found on modern maps, as at 'Nanspek', 'the muddy valley'.

In some senses settlements on the two manors described here may have been particularly badly affected. Hartland is on the poor Culm Measures and was isolated and remote, distant from any regional concentration of industry. Moreover, the manor was unlucky in lordship, for the Dynhams, who had used it as a major seat until about 1400, then moved to more accessible landscapes elsewhere in Devon.[69] In the twelfth century successive Dynham lords of Hartland may well have encouraged subdivision of holdings in order to provide further income and manpower for a military following: the 'Romance of Fouke Le Fitz Waryn' records that Josce de Dynham was able to raise 'an army and a countless number of people' from the manor.[70] Removal of the family and household from Hartland would, conversely, have taken away from their tenants an important market for the products of their holdings. Helston, likewise, had much poor, very marginal land and also suffered badly through local economic decline. Benevolent though the Duchy administration was, it could not prevent the effects of decline in tin production—part of a depression afflicting many sectors of overseas trade-on demand for farm products.[71] But many other manors shared the same types of economic difficulties as did these two, and even where farming was less depressed some shrunken settlements can be found. We certainly cannot agree with W.G.Hoskins, in one of his later writings, when he stated: 'the pattern of settlement in 1086 was virtually what it is today. There have been no significant changes'.[72] The bone structure may well have already been in place at the time of the Norman Conquest, but many of the details are as much a product of late-medieval changes as of the remoter past.

Desertion of settlement in the South West was not the work of landlords. Even in the Midlands the most recent research is tending to stress just how much the fabric of village society crumbled as a result of long-term social and economic changes during the later Middle Ages; many to-be-deserted villages were in an advanced state of decay before, in some cases, being finally depopulated by landlords.[73] In the South West, as indeed in the Midlands for much of our period, lords in fact did much to *prevent* the decay of settlements for they were increasingly becoming rentiers and needed to retain tenants rather than dismiss them. They made a substantial contribution to maintaining the human and physical fabric of settlements by paying for repairs to tenants' buildings.[74] There are references in account rolls to seigneurial repairs on many episcopal manors and a *valor* of the bishop's estate in 1484-5 sets repairs against total income on some of the Cornish properties.[75] Yet this was not simply episcopal charity, for we find the same on other estates, on those of the Duchy of Cornwall, the Dean and Chapter of Exeter and the Arundells, for example.[76] In some cases, of course, lords had no option but to sanction decay, as when a settlement was totally abandoned, or when one tenant engrossed several vacant holdings. An entry from a Stoke Fleming court roll of 1468 states that 'John Foterell takes four holdings ... yet need repair and sustain ... [only] a hall, a bakehouse and a barn', the reason being that the charges of maintaining all buildings would be too great on this engrossed holding.[77]

It was engrossing by tenants and not depopulation by landlords which led to decline in the numbers and size of settlements. By the end of the later Middle Ages large farms built up through amalgamations were for the most part enclosed, so that their occupiers experienced none of those strains of keeping an arable open-field system in viable operation which were felt in some Midland communities. There was more freedom of choice in matters of husbandry and greater opportunity to diversify towards pastoral farming. Such large, viable tenures were relatively secure from the depopulator, so that when Wolsey's commission investigated depopulation it did not see need to visit the far South West.[78]

Decline in settlement size was one by-product of the amalgamation of holdings. Another, with equally significant effects on what we see in the landscape today, was enclosure: during the later Middle Ages the South West underwent a movement towards severalty of some magnitude, which is under-estimated by those historians who begin their accounts of English enclosure around the beginning of the sixteenth century. In order to understand the size of the movement we must for a moment again retrace our steps before the Black Death. Isolated farms were not, of course, involved in open-field farming. Most of the, relatively few, nucleated villages of Devon had extensive open fields, as Finberg demonstrated.[79] In addition, the small hamlet, that dominant settlement form in the South West, was often associated with an open-field system in miniature. Elsewhere I have published references to some Devon examples.[80] For Cornwall, the evidence for hamlet open-field systems may be briefly summarized as follows. First, there are clear medieval documentary references to holdings lying *acra per acram*, or *ubique versus solem* ('everywhere towards the sun', probably implying a holding divided into strips) or *sullonatim inter vicinos* ('divided into strips among neighbours').[81] A fourteenth-century document relating to Trevia on the manor of Helstone in Trigg states that a vacant holding of fourteen and a half acres had been divided up among eleven surviving nominal holdings in the hamlet; a division into strips would have been the only feasible method and may well have been a custom going back to the origins themselves of the hamlet.[82] Second, there is excellent evidence of survivals of open-field systems after 1500, at Predannack Wollas, for example, or Blerrick, or Tolcarne or Tregurrian.[83] Third, when the farmers of a hamlet wished to use their wasteland as a sporadically cultivated outfield, as late as the nineteenth century, they were accustomed to divide it up into strips; the practice may well represent a tradition of sharing on the infields, long since enclosed.[84] Fourth, Richard Carew in his *Survey*, and the anonymous related text 'Of measuring land in Cornwayl', state that open fields were giving way to enclosures in the early sixteenth century—presumably the tail-end of the later medieval enclosure movement.[85] If one could only travel back in time into the Cornish, or the Devonshire, landscapes of about 1300 one would find a great deal of the farmland unenclosed.

Enclosure of open-field land during the later Middle Ages was, in part, a 'natural' process: as the number of farmers in a hamlet declined, and as holdings were amalgamated, so remaining tenants found themselves in possession of several adjacent strips which could then be enclosed 'by unity of possession'. But there is also a good deal of evidence for *deliberate* and calculated exchanges of strips as a prelude to enclosure. Thus when, in 1415, five tenants of Stoke Fleming paid capons to their lord for permission to exchange strips, they stated that it was 'in order to improve their holdings' (*ad meliorandum tenuras*); in 1357 two Cornish tenants urged that an exchange would be 'for the profit and convenience' of their lord; an agreement of 1394, abolishing open-field at the hamlet of Brownstone, speaks of the 'grave damage' caused by intermixture of strips.[86] Enclosure was rendered relatively easy by the small number of tenants involved at any one place; by lack of rigid arrangements for common pasture on the arable; and by the fact that use of wastes for temporary cultivation virtually ceased during the later Middle Ages, releasing extra pasture which could be used instead of common grazing on the arable.[87] In 1954 W.G. Hoskins perceptively noticed that 'in some places whole furlongs, covering several acres, seem to have been enclosed ... in other places ... we can see the fossilized strips on the 2½-inch or 6-inch map today'. The reasons for these differences, he added, 'still await detailed enquiry'.[88] An answer which might be suggested is that where the number of farmers involved in enclosure was small and diminishing, amalgamation of strips was rendered relatively easy, but where populations were larger enclosure proceeded piece by piece.[89] The larger enclosures were also more suitable for arable farming while the 'fossilized' strips of an acre or so each were ideal for careful control of livestock so that, as Hooker realized, animals 'by theire often chaunges . . . feede styll as it were upon a new springnynge grasse'.[90]

What was the motive behind enclosure? The obvious answer is that it allowed the land to be used more efficiently for both arable and pastoral farming, particularly perhaps the latter. Regional variation in the chronology of the movement certainly suggests an association with pastoral farming. Enclosure was virtually complete by 1500 in those regions which became most strongly pastoral, including much (except the south) of Devon, a county which Leland saw in the 1530s, later describing hedging in progress on Anglesey as 'after Devonshire fascion'. It proceeded more slowly in the more arable regions, including the Cornish coastlands to which Carew's observation (c. 1600) on survival of open-field husbandry 'in time not past the remembrance of some yet living' is most relevant.[91]

Pays

In his 'Synopsis Chorographical of Devonshire' John Hooker described a tract of mid Devon 'about Okehampton, Hatherley, Idesley, Chylmeyle and other places' where 'the drincke which they do make . . . [of oats] is spoyled drincke', so vile that 'what creature soever do eate or tast thereof . . . it will make him to vomyte', notwithstanding, he adds more hopefully, 'the people of that countrie beinge used thereat do endure the same very well'. Here is an extreme localism in the sixteenth century, a unique local beverage so strange that it repelled the outsider. And there is evidence for other localisms in the period with which this essay is concerned: for example, the men of Dartmoor, united by special privileges in common rights, described less fortunate men from the rest of the shire as 'outsiders'—*extranei* according to a document of 1382; a lease of 1487 describes certain agricultural practices in West Devon as 'the usage and custom of the local vicinity' (*usus et modus patrie*).[92]

Examination of the ways in which the localized practices and customs of the vicinity or *pays* (the *patria* of the lease of 1487, the *pais*[93] of Norman-French, the 'countrie' of Hooker and other sixteenth-century and seventeenth-century writers)[94] exerted a strong influence on the lives of countrymen in the past has been a fruitful theme in recent historical writing. Rural by-employments, religious beliefs, political attitudes, popular culture, field systems, vernacular architecture: all have been studied in terms of differences which were engendered by different patterns of settlement, topography and farming type, although the inter-connections between these variables still await a good deal of further research.[95] Most studied perhaps, and especially for the sixteenth and seventeenth centuries, have been the basic cultural parameters of regions, the farming types whose differing needs, rhythms and institutions lent vitality and distinctiveness to different types of *pays*.[96]

In a masterful survey of the farming regions of Tudor England Joan Thirsk emphasized the role of rising population in the sixteenth century, and a correspondingly more sophisticated market for agricultural produce, in crystallizing differences between regions: each region 'found itself exerting greater efforts to produce the food which it could grow well ... The whole country was drawn more firmly than ever before into a dovetailed system of agricultural production'.[97] What part did changes during the later Middle Ages play in the development of farming regions? Opinions vary. It has been claimed that decline in population encouraged peasant farmers to return to self-sufficient farming.[98] On the other hand, it can be argued that expansion in the size of farms, and disappearance of the manorial obligations of tenants could allow greater regional specialization, *especially* where market opportunities were present and were expanding.[99] In some cases the seeds of later specialization were being sown in the later Middle Ages, as Joan Thirsk in fact surmised.[100]

A rather crude but nevertheless telling indicator of such trends in later

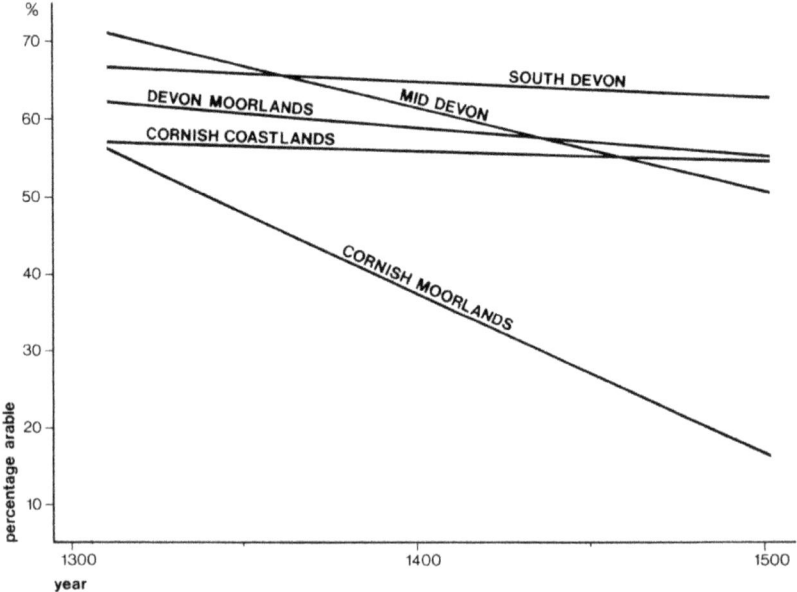

Fig. 11 Regional trends in the proportion of land used as arable, c. 1300—c. 1500. Sources: P.R.O., C.133, 134, 145 and S.C. 11/798; B.L. Harl. MSS 3660; Calendar of Inquisitions Post Mortem, Henry VII

medieval Devon and Cornwall comes from figures on land-use (Fig. 11).[101] Towards the end of the pre-plague period, in about 1300, it is remarkable how relatively little variation existed between region and region in the proportion of the land which was used as arable. What had taken place, probably during the twelfth and thirteenth centuries, was a *convergence* in land-use between region and region, as pressure of population stimulated conversion to arable of some of the most unsuitable soils of the South West: peasant farmers were pressed into grain cultivation for subsistence and for the market.[102] During the later Middle Ages, by contrast, there took place a *divergence* in the characteristics of regions, at least from the viewpoint of land-use. Everywhere the proportion of the land under arable declined, but as Fig. 11 shows, the decline was greater in some regions than in others.

The theme of regional divergence in land-use is well illustrated in the contrasting fortunes of the Cornish coastlands and the Cornish moorlands—the latter comprising Foweymoor (now 'Bodmin' Moor), Blackmore and the moory landscapes northwards and westwards of Truro in the far west.[103] At the end of the early Middle Ages, in about 1300, the proportion of the land under arable was remarkably similar in both (figures for moorland manors relate only to the 'improved' parts of demesnes, not to common land). Later there took place on the moorlands a massive reversion to pasture and waste.[104] To a degree the enormous acreages described here as 'furze and heath' in some inquisitions from the reign of Henry VII may result from over-estimates among landlords and their heirs in order to safeguard claims to toll on tin.[105] Increase in the area under waste may have been partly a result of the activities of tinners who, according to a complaint of 1361, reduced 'good land' to 'stones and gravel'.[106] But the main reason was a decline in cultivation for which good indirect evidence is provided by references to grain mills 'ruinous', 'waste' or 'fallen' around all of the Cornish moorlands.[107] In the thirteenth century the population of Cornwall and demand for foodstuffs had been great enough to encourage reclamation and cultivation of relatively unproductive soils on moorland fringes where foodstuffs could be sold directly to tinners—no doubt the reason for the stalls set up on the moory manor of Tywarnhaile.[108] But with the demand reduced during the fourteenth century the more easily worked soils of the coastlands became the main producers of grain with, consequently, little decline in the proportion of arable. Cultivation there was relatively easy and was made even more profitable by closeness to sea-sand and the presence of markets both in numerous ports, including Plymouth, and inland in the moorland stannaries which, by virtue of the narrow configuration of the county, were always close to hand.[109] With total demand for grains reduced, cultivation on the

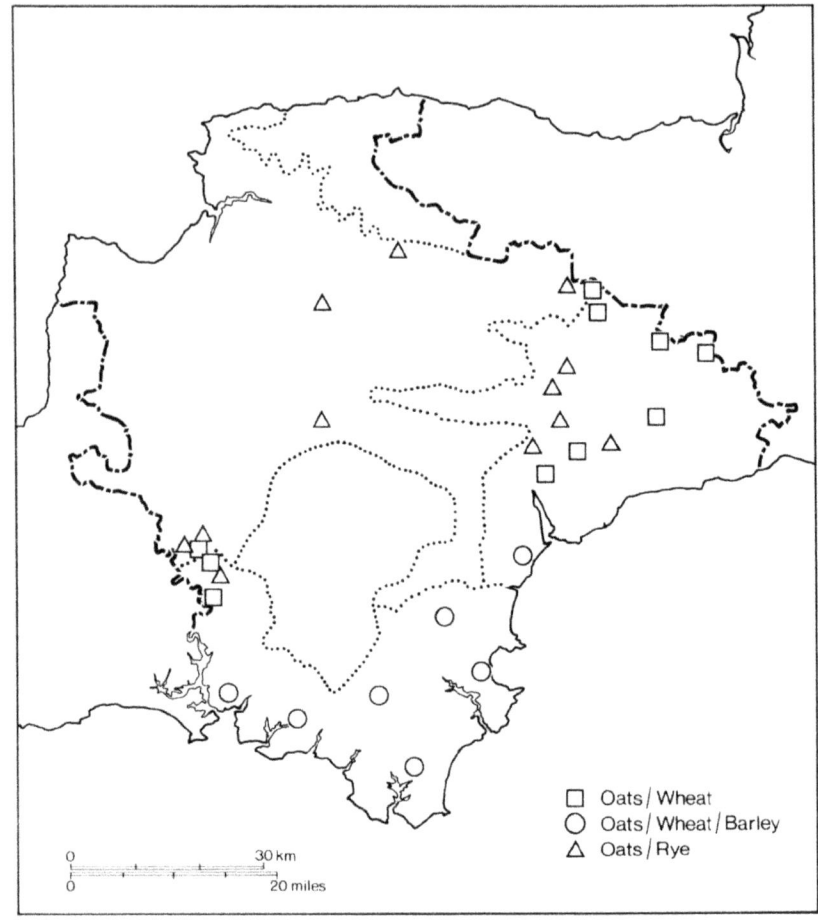

Fig. 12   Crop combinations. Sources: manorial accounts, C.14th and C.15th

moorlands—more arduous and costly, producing poorer yields of the poorer varieties of crops—was bound to suffer.

Specialisms, as they developed during the later Middle Ages, involved more than a separation of regions into the arable and the pastoral, for there was regional specialization too *within* each of those sectors. Figs. 12 and 13 provide some rough indicators. The first map shows crops recorded in demesne accounts for the most part dating from between 1350 and 1400.

Peasant farmers, patterns of settlement and pays 61

Two examples of regional specialization may be pointed to, the first in central Devon where the staple crops were rye and oats, both suited to poor soils and a damp climate. Sources not mapped on Fig. 12 show that rye dominated multure payments at Nympton and oats predominated in tithe at Hartland. At Hockford the miller's rent was rye in kind.[110] All of the evidence suggests that as cultivation was pushed forward on these poor lands during the early

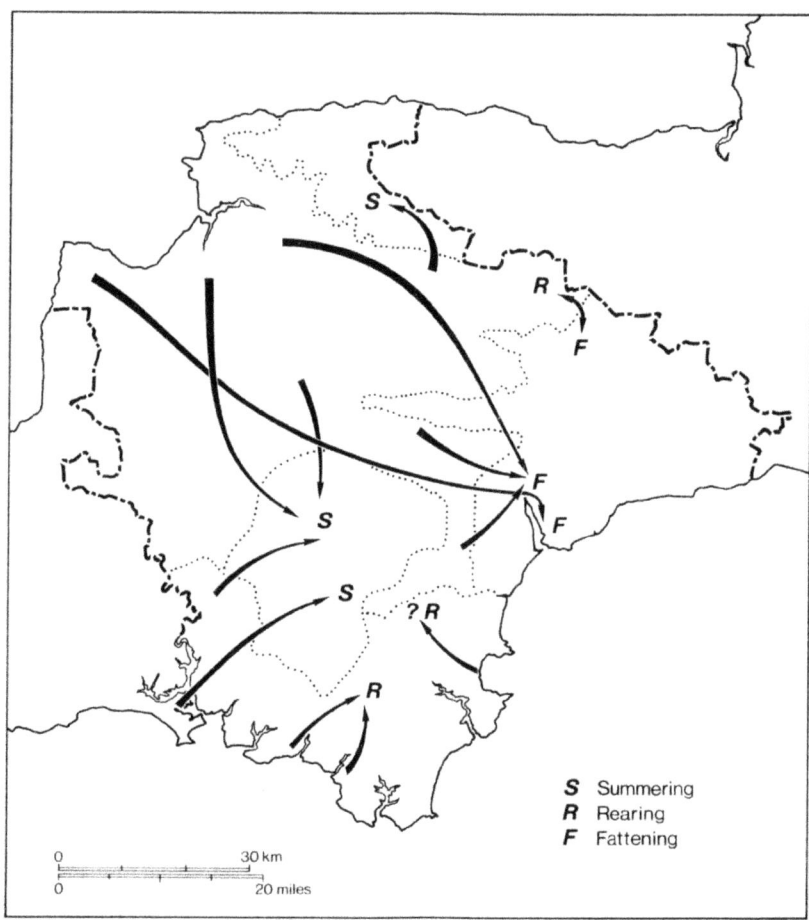

Fig. 13 Tentative examples of movements of cattle. Sources: manorial accounts and other miscellaneous documents, C.14th and C.15th

Middle Ages, oats and rye became entrenched in local diet, and remained so, sown largely for home consumption, on much reduced arable acreages after the mid-fourteenth century. Rye was the main bread grain, most usual in liveries paid to manorial workmen and used for the 'grey' loaves given by lords to their men at feast-times or to the poor.[111] Beer might even be made of rye, but the most usual ingredient was oats (also used in pottage), to produce the unpalatable special brew described earlier.[112] Fig. 12 reveals a second regional specialization, barley growing in south Devon. Farmers in the region sowed a mix of crops (wheat and barley as well as oats) far more profitable than that of central Devon, these high-priced and high-yielding grains reflecting a less 'coarse' local diet: rye bread and oatmeal seem to be disappearing from tables around the end of the fourteenth century. Such changes probably reflect the position of south Devon, Leland's 'frutefulest part of all Devonshire', as a major source of grain for sale—emphases in diet following commercial trends—and the 'high class' nature of demand in the ports along the coast.[113]

Fig. 13, relating to movements of cattle, is of more speculative construction, for manorial accounts give only occasional hints about the subject; only a sample of movements, unrepresentative perhaps, is shown on the map. Movements involving the summering of cattle on Dartmoor (S on the map: four sample routes only shown) are the best documented, for the annual accounts of the Duchy of Cornwall give figures for the beasts pastured there, over 10,000 head of cattle alone in 1404.[114] Coastal manors with herds of cows but relatively few young stock, the latter being sent elsewhere for rearing after a quick weaning (R on the map), probably specialized in dairying.[115] But perhaps the most interesting specialism—because it marks the germs of what was to become a nationally renowned development—was the rise of cattle rearing in central Devon and north Devon. Herds kept not principally for dairying but for rearing are clearly identifiable in manorial accounts because they are characterized by many young animals of one, two or three years old, all making their way rung by rung up the ladder which ended, eventually, in sale for hide and meat. Such patterns of management could result in herds of impressive size, the Bishop's of ninety-six at Nympton, for example, or the ninety-eight kept by John Blake, a very minor landlord, at Hayne in the same parish.[116] A bullock-herd employed by the Bishop at his home farm near Exeter had been brought from north Devon, and Leland noted a 'very good broode of catelle' at Hartland—references indicating a special esteem for expertise in, and the products of, rearing in the region. The breed (red in colour) was nurtured in the best enclosed pastures around the farmstead and then ran on the region's many local moors, sometimes becoming virtually wild.[117] There are hints of movements of cattle (F on the map) from the region to the lusher pastures of east Devon, presumably for fattening and access to the meat and leather markets around Exeter.[118] Development of rearing took place in parallel with a sharp decline in cultivation and with certain demographic developments which no doubt gave the region its own distinctive social composition: large, widely spaced pastoral farms, few cottagers, living-in servants and—as a result of all these characteristics—very low densities of population.[119]

Development of specialisms at a regional level during the later Middle Ages has been noticed by a few other writers. Hare, for example, in his work on later medieval Wiltshire, noted 'a growing divergence between the rural economies of the county's two main regions' while Langdon, studying beasts of traction, concluded that 'regional variation ... remained somewhat shapeless until the fifteenth century when it finally began to attain the complexity it would show a century later'.[120] Lying behind these developments must have been the mechanism of the market, for it is unlikely that the great cattle herds of central Devon and of the Cornish moorlands (to take two examples) were for consumption on the farm. And, in Devon and Cornwall, the presence of abundant market outlets for farm products during the later Middle Ages is not hard to discern. One outlet was provided by labourers in the stannaries who probably made up a growing proportion of those who worked for tin in this period. Another was the urban market. Devon and Cornwall supported more boroughs than almost any other English county and the majority of them survived the later Middle Ages as small towns or 'industrial villages'; some may even have expanded, as Exeter certainly did to become England's sixth wealthiest city by the early sixteenth century.[121] The diversified economy of the South West—tinning, silver mining, cloth production, quarrying for slate, stone and lime, leather working, fishing—did not fail to stimulate the market in agricultural produce, and that stimulus seems to have encouraged regional specialization in farming.[122] Where markets were close to hand and the land fit for commercial grain production (for example, in south Devon and on the Cornish coastlands), arable specialisms developed; where markets were distant and the land poor (as in central Devon, which lacked many boroughs and industries) all was not lost, for the rearing of cattle, a mobile commodity, provided the solution, just as some of the higher and more remote regions of midland England went over to sheep farming in this period.[123] But not all of the regions of poorer land fell down to grass. Dartmoor is a good example, for there was little decline in arable farming on the moorland border farms and relatively little desertion of settlement during the fourteenth and fifteenth centuries: in this case late colonisation in the more expansive centuries of the early Middle Ages was not followed by widespread contraction and desertion after 1350, for the 'commercialization' of the moor helped to bolster demand for farm products.[124]

Having suggested that regional specialisms were beginning to develop in the later Middle Ages, to be intensified as numbers of people and demand grew in Tudor England, we should retrace our steps for the last time to the twelfth and thirteenth centuries to ask why rising population at that time did not also encourage specialization. Fig. 11 (above) certainly indicates that in thirteenth-century Devon and Cornwall there were no major contrasts in land-use between region and region; and the same kind of finding comes from research elsewhere, from Postan's work on peasant farming in Wiltshire where 'distinction between pastoral and non-pastoral villages ... turns out to be something of a phantom' in the early thirteenth century, and from Dyer's work on Warwickshire where differences in land-use between Arden and the Feldon were more muted in the early fourteenth century than they ever had been or were to be again.[125] This is not to deny a degree of specialization in the early Middle Ages, for the managers of large estates with scattered demesnes had, from a very early period, concentrated certain types of farm production on certain manors, and peasant farmers, too, faced with the need to survive and to pay rents and taxes, must have sown whichever crop would be to their greatest profit and well-being, according to the nature of their land.[126] But acute specialization, particularly in one of the branches of livestock husbandry, and of a kind which made some regions deficient in the means of subsistence, does not seem to have been a feature of the early Middle Ages.[127] One reason for this was the prevailing size of holdings which were generally too small to allow the building up of commercial flocks or herds; another, in an age of population pressure, was the need for farmers first and foremost to produce the basic subsistence for the family, grains for breads and pottages; another may well have been the way in which seigneurial exactions stifled initiative. Only when pressures of population were relaxed, during the period covered by this paper, and when other burdens of a feudal nature gradually withered away, did more choices become available: the stage was now set for the emergence of nascent farming regions each with its own attendant type of social composition.

Notes

1. H.S.A. Fox, 'Occupation of the land', 'Farming techniques' and 'Peasant farming', in E. Miller (ed.), *The Agrarian History of England and Wales, III, 1349-1500* (Cambridge University Press, forthcoming). The Research Board of the University of Leicester contributed towards the expenses.
2. M.M. Postan, 'Medieval agrarian society in its prime: England', in Postan (ed.), *The Cambridge Economic History of Europe, I, The Agrarian Life of the Middle Ages*

(1966), 550; W.G. Hoskins, 'The making of the agrarian landscape', in W.G. Hoskins and H.P.R. Finberg, *Devonshire Studies* (1952), 321; W.G.V. Balchin, *Cornwall: An Illustrated Essay on the History of the Landscape* (1954), 40.
3. M. Bloch, *Les Caractères Originaux de L'Histoire Rurale Française* (1931), 5-17; H.S.A. Fox, 'Some ecological dimensions of medieval field systems', in K. Biddick (ed.), *Archaeological Approaches to Medieval Europe* (Western Michigan University, Studies in Medieval Culture, XVIII, 1984), 134-6.
4. J.E.B. Gover, A. Mawer and F.M. Stenton, *The Place-names of Devon* (1931-2), I, xx; Hoskins, 'Agrarian landscape' (note 2), 298. For Hoskins's revised views see his *Human Geography of the South West* (1968), 6-8 and 'The Highland Zone in Domesday Book', in his *Provincial England* (1965), 15-52.
5. H.P.R. Finberg, 'The Treable charter', in his *Early Charters of Devon and Cornwall* (Department of English Local History, University of Leicester, Occasional Papers, 2, 1953), 20-31 and 'Sherborne, Glastonbury and the expansion of Wessex', *Trans. Royal Hist. Soc.*, 5th ser., 3 (1953), 109 (my own work on the period suggests that it is going too far to describe Finberg's suggestions on Celtic land units as 'an edifice of antiquarian speculation': S.M. Pearce, *The Kingdom of Dumnonia* (1978), 168); C. Thomas, 'The end of the Roman South-West', in K. Branigan and P.J. Fowler (eds.), *The Roman West County* (1976), 210-13; Pearce, *Kingdom of Dumnonia* (1978) and 'The early church in the landscape: the evidence from North Devon', *Arch. J.*, 142 (1985), 255-75; B.L. Olson and O. Padel, 'A tenth-century list of Cornish parochial saints', *Cambridge Medieval Celtic Studies*, 12 (1986), 33-71.
6. I do not mean to belittle entirely the West Saxon and early medieval contribution: there is enough regional diversity in the South West to allow considerable contributions from these periods to the making of the landscape.
7. C. Creighton, *A History of Epidemics in Britain* (1894), I, 116; J.F.D. Shrewsbury, *A History of Bubonic Plague in the British Isles* (1970), 38; M. Prestwich, *The Three Edwards* (1980), 255; Duchy of Cornwall Office (hereafter D.C.O.), roll 4 for severe pestilence in Cornwall 'before the feast of Easter', 1349; J.H. Harvey (ed.), *William Worcestre Itineraries* (1969), 94-5 for pestilence at Bodmin 'a little before Christmas', 1348.
8. T. Rogers, *A History of Agriculture and Prices in England* (1866-1902), I, 601-2.
9. D. and S. Lysons, *Magna Britannia . . . Cornwall* (1814), 33; *Cal.Close Rolls, 1377-81*, 54; *Register of the Black Prince*, II, 63-4; J. Hatcher, *English Tin Production and Trade before 1550* (1973), 90-91 and *Cal. Close Rolls, 1360-64*, 220; D.C.O., Haveners' Accounts (e.g. roll 13); D.C.O., 4 (Tywarnhaile), P.R.O., S.C., 6/828/21 (S. Teign), Longleat House MSS, 1 and 122 (Uplyme).
10. G. Twigg, *The Black Death: A Biological Reappraisal* (1984); this theory is not universally accepted.
11. Postan, 'Medieval agrarian society' (note 2), 559, 570; L.B. Larking (ed.), *The Knights Hospitallers in England* (Camden Soc., old ser., 65, 1857), 13 for Bodmiscombe; P.R.O., C. 133/122/12 for Truthall and G. Oliver, *Monasticon Dioecesis Exoniensis* (1846), 430 for Cargoll; J. Hatcher, *Rural Economy and Society in the Duchy of Cornwall 1300-1500* (1970), 96.
12. J.R. Maddicott, *The English Peasantry and the Demands of the Crown 1294-1341*

(Past and Present Society, Supplements, 1, 1975), 15; Longleat House MSS, Shapwick court rolls.
13. J. Hatcher, *Plague, Population and the English Economy 1348-1530* (1977), 58-61; idem, 'Mortality in the fifteenth century: some new evidence', *Econ. Hist. Rev.*, 2nd ser., 39 (1986), 25-31; C. Dyer, *Lords and Peasants in a changing Society* (1980), 225-8; Fox, 'Peasant farming'.
14. R.M. Smith, 'Hypothèses sur la nuptualité en Angleterre aux XIIIe—XIVe siècles', *Annales, Économies, Sociétés, Civilisations*, 38 (1983), 130-131; A. Kussmaul, *Servants in Husbandry in Early Modern England* (1981), 20.
15. The figures are, of course, very problematic. They are based on the latest estimates for *c.* 1300 and *c.* 1540: R.M. Smith, 'Human resources', in G. Astill and A. Grant (eds), *The Countryside of Medieval England* (1988), 191; E.A. Wrigley and R.S. Schofield, *The Population History of England 1541-1871: A Reconstruction* (1981), 563-9. Quotation from C.A. Sneyd (ed.), *Relation of the island of England* (Camden Soc., old. ser., 37, 1847), 31.
16. P.L. Hull (ed.), *The Caption of Seisin of the Duchy of Cornwall (1377)* (Devon and Cornwall Record Society, new ser., 17, 1971), 12-23; P.R.O., E. 132/152B; P. Herring, 'An Exercise in Landscape History: Pre-Norman and Medieval Brown Willy and Bodmin Moor, Cornwall' (unpubl. M. Phil. thesis, University of Sheffield, 1986), II, 13.
17 For example, H.E. Hallam, *Settlement and Society: A Study of the Early Agrarian History of South Lincolnsnhire* (1965), 216.
18. P.R.O., S.C. 6/828/21.
19. Dean and Chapter Archives, Exeter (hereafter D.C.A), 4798-4835; D.R.O., 902M/M9-31; P.R.O., E. 306/2/7 as an example of an assessment roll with many vacant holdings.
20. D.C.A., 4834; P.R.O. S.C. 11/765 wrongly ascribed to Ric.II and Huntington Library, San Marino, Hastings MSS, HAM 64, rental wrongly ascribed to 1577.
21. Hatcher, *Rural Economy* (note 11), 229-35, 249-52 and Fox, 'Peasant farming'.
22. Hartland and Stokenham in Devon, Helston in Kirrier, Helstone in Trigg and Tybesta in Cornwall: P.R.O., C. 133/102/2 collated with Arundell MSS (in private hands, hereafter Arundell), R. & S. 5 and D.R.O., Survey of Lord Dynham's lands; P.R.O., S.C. 11/765 and 168; Hull, *Caption* (note 16) and P.R.O., E. 306/2/14 and 2/16 for the Cornish manors. For the total rentals at Helstone in Trigg and Tybesta, see Hatcher, *Rural Economy* (note 11), 264.
23. R.J. Faith, 'Peasant families and inheritance customs in medieval England', *Agric. Hist. Rev.*, 14 (1966), 86-92; R.M. Smith, 'Some issues concerning families and their property in rural England 1250-1800', in idem (ed.), *Land, Kinship and Lifecycle* (1984), 58-62.
24. B.L. Harl. MS. 4766; Fox, 'Peasant farming'.
25. P.R.O., E. 306/2/1 and D.C.O., 475. For the Duchy estate at large, Hatcher, *Rural Economy* (note 11), 220.
26. This suggestion, for Mendip lead-mining communities, is made by I. Blanchard, 'Industrial employment and the rural land market, 1380-1520', in Smith, *Land, Kinship and Lifecycle* (note 23), 245.
27. J. Hatcher, 'Non-manorialism in medieval Cornwall', *Agric. Hist. Rev.*, 18

(1970), 1-16; P.R.O., E. 306/2/6 and S.C. 11/151, D.R.O., W1258M/E/24, B.L. Add. rolls 64391, 64534 (Bishopric estate); Arundell R. & S. 9 (court roll on dorse) and M.A. 34 (Tregarne and Lambroun) for the Arundell estate; P.R.O., S.C. 6/822/17 and D.R.O., W1258M/E/23 (for other lordships); Fox, 'Peasant farming' (note 1).
28. P.R.O., S.C. 11/765; Huntington Library, Hastings MSS, HAM 64, rental of '1577', P.R.O., S.C. 11/168.
29. It must also be noted that for a farm to change hands from a person with surname 'a' to an occupier with surname 'b' does not necessarily mean that it has passed out of the family; b could be a married daughter or a cousin. But the very infrequency of succession of farms from fathers to sons makes much succession to more distant kin unlikely.
30. For the possibilities which exist for the use of surname evidence see, for example, R. McKinley, *The Surnames of Oxfordshire* (English Surnames Series, III, 1977), 69-80.
31. Fox, 'Peasant farming'.
32. See the surveys of Devonshire farmhouses, by N.W. Alcock, S.R.Jones and C. Hulland, *Trans. Dev. Assn.*, 100 (1968)-116 (1984); Fox, 'Peasant farming'. A good number of surviving farmhouses from this first 'great rebuilding' are being identified in the Department of the Environment's new lists.
33. The terminology is very debatable. See, for example, A. Macfarlane, *The Origins of English Individualism* (1978), 7-33.
34. P.R.O., S.C. 6/830/29 and *c.f.* C. 134/16/9; Hull, *Caption* (note 16), 114-5; P.R.O., C. 134/99 and *Cal. Misc. Inq.*, 1387-93, 89; Arundell, R. & S. 1 and 8; D.R.O., DD. 54916. See also N.W. Alcock, 'An East Devon manor in the later Middle Ages, Part II', *Trans. Dev. Assn.*, 105 (1973), 159.
35. H.P.R. Finberg, *Tavistock Abbey: A Study in the Social and Economic History of Devon* (1951), 252; Hatcher, *Rural Economy* (note 11), 291.
36. Following the definition of Kussmaul, *Servants* (note 14), 135: a 'servant in husbandry' was 'hired by the year, lived with his or her master, and was unmarried'.
37. *Ibid.*, 168 and Smith, 'Hypothèses' (note 14), 130-1.
38. D.R.O., Cary MSS, rental of 1523 and T.L. Stoate (ed.), *Devon Lay Subsidy Rolls 1524-7* (1979), 134-5. These men were assessed at £1 on 'goods', but such assessments in the Devon subsidy often conceal labourers working for wages (for example, *ibid.*, 11, 121). At Trelawne in Pelynt a rental of 1523-4 lists no cottagers yet the subsidy for the parish reveals twelve labourers: P.R.O., E. 315/385 and T.L. Stoate (ed.), *Cornwall Subsidies in the Reign of Henry VIII* (1985), 107.
39. P.R.O., S.C. 11/765 and Huntington Library, Hastings MSS, HAM 64, rental of 1577. I would like to record here my debt to Mr. W.A. Roberts of Stonkeham for much help and hospitality.
40. For example, P.R.O., S.C. 11/171; D.R.O. Cary MSS, Stoke Fleming survey of *c.* 1523; Royal Institution of Cornwall, HB/20/12. For a possible case of a husbandman taking on a cottage in addition to his land, at Uthnoe in Cornwall, see S.R.O., DD. WO 47/3, account of 1438-9.

41. D.R.O., Cary MSS, Ashwater court roll of Oct. 1436. For similar movements see D.C.A., 4802 (from Sidbury 'to eastern parts', presumably the more arable areas of Somerset) and D.R.O. 314M/M/2 (from Bratton Clovelly 'away from the county').
42. J. Hatcher, 'Myths, miners and agricultural communities' and I. Blanchard, 'Rejoinder: *stannator fabulosus*', *Agric. Hist. Rev.*, 22 (1974), 54-61, 62-74; the debate could perhaps be resolved by postulating a chronological shift from reliance on one form of labour to reliance on the other.
43. For labour in the stannaries, Hatcher, *English Tin Production* (note 9), 43-88.
44. This is not to deny stratification among labourers in the thirteenth century, as my work on the poor on the Glastonbury estate in Somerset will demonstrate.
45. J. Hall and A. Hamlin, 'Deserted medieval settlements in Devon', *Devon Historian*, 13 (1976), 2.
46. Helston in Kirrier, Helstone in Trigg and Tybesta: sources as in note 22 above. Carminowe, Tregarne, Trembleathe, Treloy, Lanherne, Connerton, Lanhadron, Bodwannick: Arundell, R. & S. 14. Cargoll and Tregaire: D.R.O., W1258/E/24 and 382/ER/2. Charles Henderson rightly claimed that there were no true medieval villages in Cornwall: *Essays in Cornish History* (1963), 19.
47. H.S.A. Fox, 'The field systems of East and South Devon. Part 1: East Devon', *Trans. Dev. Assn.*, 104 (1972), 113; *The Anglo-Saxon Chronicle*, trans. G.N. Garmonsway (1972 paperback edition), 48.
48. See the proper strictures on my earlier work in Herring, 'An exercise in Landscape History' (note 16), I, 5-6. Hoskins noted the importance of the hamlet type: 'Highland Zone' (note 4), 50-51.
49. Arundell, R. & S. 5—figures relate to that part of the manor of Hartland which the rental allows us to recreate; Hull, *Caption* (note 16), 58-61.
50. As note 49.
51. P.R.O., E. 132/152B. The hamlet at Brown Willy originated in the same way: Herring, 'An Exercise in Landscape History' (note 16), II, 2-10.
52. For example, B.L. Add. MS 28, 838 f.129 v. and D.C.A., 2937; D.R.O., 902M/M/32.
53. The Irish and Welsh parallels are very instructive: E.E.Evans, 'The ecology of peasant life in Western Europe', in W.L. Thomas (ed.), *Man's Role in Changing the Face of the Earth* (1956), 231 for a suggested model for the co-existence of raths and clachans in Ireland; V.B. Proudfoot, 'The economy of the Irish rath', *Med. Arch.*, 5 (1961), 119 for the same; idem, 'Clachans in Ireland', *Gwerin*, 2 (1959), 111-5; G.R.J. Jones, 'Some medieval rural settlements in North Wales', *Trans. Inst. Brit. Geog.*, 19 (1953), 51-72. For 'defended' and 'undefended' settlements in Dark Age Cornwall see C. Thomas, 'The character and origins of Roman Dumnonia', in C. Thomas (ed.), *Rural Settlement in Roman Britain* (1966), 91, 97.
54. By S. Baring-Gould, D. Dudley and E.M.Minter, G. Beresford and D. Austin. See also, C.D. Linehan, 'Deserted sites and rabbit-warrens on Dartmoor, Devon', *Med. Arch.*, 10 (1966), 113-44, although a considerable number of the sites there listed were deserted in post-medieval periods.
55. E.M. Jope and R.I. Threlfall, 'Excavation of a medieval settlement at Beere, North

Tawton, Devon', *Med. Arch.*, 2 (1958), 112-40; R. Bridgewater and T. Miles, 'A trial excavation at Kigbeare, Okehampton Hamlets', *Proc. Dev. Arch. Soc.*, 36 (1978), 241-4; G. Beresford, 'Tresmorn, St. Gennys', *Cornish Arch.*, 10 (1971), 55-73; the checklists for Creed and Morwestow, *Cornish Arch.*, 7 (1968) and 14 (1975). A good many sites now deserted today became so relatively recently, through some of the same kinds of forces—amalgamation of farms, decay of cottages—described here for the later Middle Ages. For some descriptions of later desertion see C. Vancouver, *General View of the Agriculture of the County of Devon* (1808), 93-4, 98; W.G. Hoskins, 'The occupation of land in Devonshire, 1650-1800', *Devon. Corn. N. Q.*, 21 (1940-41), 5-7; C. Michell and M. Common, 'Staunton—a deserted South Hams village', *Devon Historian*, 16 (1978), 21-4. Hennard, at the Roadford site, probably falls into this category.
56. D.R.O., C.R. 473, 481 and 382/ER/2; B.L. Add. roll 64536; P.R.O. E. 306/2/6.
57. M. Aston, 'Deserted farmsteads on Exmoor and the lay subsidy of 1327 in West Somerset', *Proc. Som. Arch. Nat. Hist. Soc.*, 127 (1983), 71-104.
58. Gover, Mawer and Stenton, *Place-names of Devon* (note 4), I, 324 and II, 505.
59. It is thus far easier to use south-western rentals and extents for the reconstruction of settlement fabric than it is to use those from 'the land of villages' for the same purpose, though see P.D.A. Harvey, 'Mapping the village: the historical evidence', in D. Hooke (ed.), *Medieval Villages* (1985), 36-41.
60. Arundell, R. & S. 5; assession rolls were first used in settlement studies by M.W. Beresford, 'Dispersed and grouped settlement in medieval Cornwall', *Agric. Hist. Rev.*, 12 (1964), 13-27.
61. For example, Record Commission, *Record of Caernarvon* (1838); J.W. Willis-Bund (ed.), *The Black Book of St. David's* (1902).
62. The following paragraphs are based upon Arundell, R. & S. 5, P.R.O., C. 133/89 and 102, 135/32, 139/40 and 170, Arundell, M.A. 225-41, D.R.O., Survey of Lord Dynham's land and 1201A/PW3 (an Easter book which helps with identification of holdings). The ditty is from R.P. Chope, *The Book of Hartland* (1940), 8. My map reconstructs only that part of Hartland manor included in the rental of *c.* 1365, sections of which have been torn away.
63. For other examples see Fox, 'Occupation of the land'.
64. H.S.A. Fox, 'Contraction: desertion and dwindling of dispersed settlement in a Devon parish', *Annual Report of the Medieval Village Research Group*, 31 (1983), 41.
65. Following paragraphs based upon Hull, *Caption* (note 16), 84-91, P.R.O., E. 306/2/1, 2, 12 and 14, S.C. 6/816/12, 817/1, 3, 8, 18, C.R.O., assessionable map of Helston in Kirrier. See also P.L.Hull, 'Richard Carew's discourse about the Duchy suit, 1594', *J. Royal Inst. Cornwall*, new ser., 4 (1962), 195. I would like to record here my thanks to Oliver Padel of the Institute of Cornish Studies for help in identifying place-names in Helston and for much other cheerful assistance.
66. There is, of course, the possibility that the tenant to whom the chase was farmed sub-let holdings within this area. For a list of tenements in the chase see, for example, P.R.O., S.C. 6/817/8.
67. Carnebone was temporarily deserted during the 1460's, but was later reoccupied

by a single tenant who also farmed the 'waste' site of Garlidna, still 'a waste called Carlynnowe' in the mid-sixteenth century.
68. J. Norden, *The Surveyors Dialogue* (1607).
69. In 1391 the 'lord and lady and their *familia*' paid for 42 cart-loads of victuals and necessaries to be transported to Kingskerswell, almost certainly removal expenses: Arundell, M.A. 225. Martin Cherry, to whose stimulating conversation I owe much, tells me that in the fifteenth century the family lived largely at Kingskerswell and Nutwell.
70. J. Stevenson (ed.), *Radulphi de Coggeshall Chronicon Anglicanum* (1875), 306. Editors of the most recent edition write of the 'mainly accurate local history' in Fouke: E.J. Hathaway *et al.* (eds.), *Fouke le Fitz Waryn* (Anglo-Norman Text Society, 1975), xxxiii.
71. Hatcher, *Rural Economy* (note 11), 95-8, 111-2, 125-6,150, 163; idem, *English Tin Production* (note 9), 91, 116.
72. Hoskins, 'Highland Zone' (note 4), 45.
73. C. Dyer, 'Deserted medieval villages in the West Midlands', *Econ. Hist. Rev.*, 2nd ser., 35 (1982), 19-34; R.H. Hilton, 'Villages désertés et histoire économique: recherches françaises et anglaises', *Études Rurales*, 32 (1968), 107-8.
74. Dyer, 'Deserted medieval villages' (note 73), 27-8.
75. For example, B.L. Add. rolls 64392, 64546, D.R.O., C.R. 470, W1258M/E/24, a/c of 1399-1400; N.W. Alcock, 'The medieval cottages of Bishops Clyst, Devon', *Med. Arch.*, 9 (1965), 146-53.
76. Fox, 'Peasant farming'.
77. D.R.O., 902M/M/22.
78. M.W. Beresford, *The Lost Villages of England* (1954), 218.
79. H.P.R. Finberg, 'The open field in Devon', in Hoskins and Finberg, *Devonshire Studies* (note 2), 265-88.
80. H.S.A. Fox, 'The chronology of enclosure and economic development in medieval Devon', *Econ. Hist. Rev.*, 2nd ser., 28 (1975), 186, n. 2 (Ogbear), n. 6 (Keyberry), 187 n. 2 (Aunk), none of which places was a village or large manorial centre. Further examples of Devon hamlets with open-field systems are Weston in Awliscombe, Dunnabridge, Challacombe, Swannaton in Stoke Fleming and Brownstone: D.R.O. 123M/E/31 and later surveys; P.R.O., S.C. 12/30/27; D.R.O., 1508M/surveys/vol. 7; D.R.O., 902M/M/3; D.R.O., Z1/10/26. See also Finberg, 'The open field' (note 79), 279-81.
81. Royal Institution of Cornwall, Henderson transcripts vol. 19/314 and 26/67 (Trevellion in Luxulyan); C.R.O., DDME/Treworyan deeds no.1 (Treworyan in Probus); C.R.O., DD. Carylon no. 175 (Little Lantyan in Lostwithiel); J.H.Rowe (ed.), *Cornwall Feet of Fines*, I (1914), 48 Boduel in Liskeard).
82. P.R.O., E. 306/2/1.
83. C.R.O., Gwithian tithe map and DDX/101/5; map in Lanhydrock Atlas, Lanhydrock House; C.R.O., DDME/Landrake survey; Arundell, R. & S. 42; P.R.O., E. 315/388.
84. H.S.A. Fox, 'Outfield cultivation in Devon and Cornwall: a reinterpretation', in M. Havinden (ed.), *Husbandry and Marketing in the South-West 1500-1800* (Exeter Papers in Economic History, 8, 1973), 31 and n. 4.

85. *Survey of Cornwall* (ed. F.E. Halliday, 1953), 138; B.L. Cott. MS, Faust. E. V., which certainly seems to be related to Carew, for certain themes and phrases are common to both writings. A fifth type of evidence, the morphological evidence of fossilized strips in enclosed field patterns, is also important: A.H. Shorter, W.L.D. Ravenhill, K.J. Gregory, *South West England* (1969), 135 and P. Flatrès, *Géographie rurale de quatre contrées celtiques: Irlande, Galles, Cornwall & Man* (1957), 349-70.
86. D.R.O., 902M/M/13; *Register of the Black Prince*, II, 129; D.R.O., Z1/10/26. For other references to exchange and enclosure see Fox, 'Chronology' (note 80), 186-7; P.R.O., S.C. 2/167/46 (Otterton); D.C.A., 4807 (Sidbury); D.R.O., 1334M/M/1 (Sidmouth); A.M. Erskine, 'Evidence of open field cultivation in Culmstock', *Devon Cornw. N. Q.*, 32 (1971-3), 161-3.
87. Fox, 'Outfield cultivation' (note 84), 33.
88. W.G. Hoskins, *Devon* (1954), 73.
89. Based upon arguments in Fox, 'Chronology' (note 80), 194-8 and 'Field systems' (note 47), 125.
90. M.J. Blake, 'Hooker's Synopsis Chorographical of Devonshire', *Trans. Devon. Assn.* 47 (1915), 344.
91. Fox, 'Chronology' (note 80),186-7; H.S.A. Fox, 'A Study of the Field Systems of Devon and Cornwall' (unpubl. Ph.D. thesis, University of Cambridge, 1971), 62 and Fig. 2.1 for survival of open field on the Cornish coastlands; *Leland's Itinerary in England and Wales*, ed. L.T. Smith (1964 edn), III, 90; Carew, *Survey* (note 85), 138.
92. Blake, 'Hooker's Synopsis' (note 90), 345; P.R.O., C. 145/224/3; D.R.O. W1258M/D/53/124.
93. See, for example, D. Oschinsky, *Walter of Henley and Other Treatises on Estate Management and Accounting* (1971), 314.
94. See, for example, J. Aubrey, *The Natural History of Wiltshire*, ed. J. Britton (1847), 11; W. Camden, *Britannia* (1610 edn.), 561.
95. J. Thirsk, 'Industries in the countryside', in F.J. Fisher (ed.), *Essays in the Economic and Social History of Tudor and Stuart England in Honour of R.H. Tawney* (1961), 70-88; A. Everitt, *The Pattern of Rural Dissent: The Nineteenth Century* (Department of English Local History, University of Leicester, Occasional Papers, 2nd ser., 4, 1972), 45-6; D. Underdown, 'The chalk and the cheese: contrasts among the English Clubmen', *Past and Present*, 85 (1979), 25-48; D. Underdown, *Revel, Riot and Rebellion: Popular Politics and Culture in England 1603-1660* (1985), 73-105; H.S.A. Fox, 'The people of the wolds in English settlement history', in *The Rural Settlements of Medieval England* (forthcoming); M.W. Barley, *The English Farmhouse and Cottage* (1961), 82.
96. J. Thirsk, 'The farming regions of England', in J. Thirsk (ed.), *The Agrarian History of England and Wales*, IV, *1500-1640* (1967), 1-112 and also her *England's Agricultural Regions and Agrarian History, 1500-1750* (1987); E. Kerridge, *The Agricultural Revolution* (1967), 41-180.
97. Thirsk, 'Farming regions', (note 96), 3.
98. W.G. Hoskins, 'Regional farming in England', *Agric. Hist. Rev.*, 2 (1954), 7.
99. Fox, 'Peasant farming'.

100. Thirsk, 'Farming regions', (note 96), 1 and *England's Agricultural Regions* (note 96), 16.
101. The lines on Fig. 11 have been drawn to join percentage figures from a sample of inquisitions 1295-1325 to figures from a sample of inquisitions 1497-1509, and should not be used to draw conclusions about the relative steepness in the decline of arable from region to region.
102. *c.f.* Postan's findings for Wiltshire mentioned later in this section.
103. For other examples see Fox, 'Occupation of the land'.
104. A good example is the new chase at Helston in Kirrier, for which see the previous section.
105. For example, the inquisition on Richard Nanfant, *Cal. I.P.M. Hen. VII*, III, 226-8.
106. *Register of the Black Prince*, II, 178.
107. Arundell, M.A. 29 (Bodardle); M.A. 5 (Cardinham); P.R.O., S.C. 6/1138/2 and D.R.O., W1258M/E/24 (Cargoll); Arundell, R. & S. 8, 14 (Carminowe); P.R.O., S.C. 6/823/28 (Hamatethy); Arundell, M.A. 34 (Lambroun); P.R.O., C. 139/103 and S.C. 6/823/38 (Merthen); P.R.O., S.C. 6/823/38 (Trelowith).
108. Hull, *Caption* (note 16), 83.
109. Barley, a demanding grain whose cultivation was restricted in the late medieval South West to the most fertile soils was sown on the Cornish coastlands: D.R.O., C.R. 435 and B.L. Add. rolls 64391-2 (Burniere); D.R.O., W1258M/E/24 (Cargoll); P.R.O., E. 106/6/11 (Trevennen and 'St. Cadix'); *Register of the Black Prince*, II, 178 and 32-3 (place uncertain and Roseworthy); P.R.O., S.C. 6/822/8 (Callington ?); Arundell, M.A. 56 (St. Columb mill). Arable land was particularly highly valued on the coastlands, at 10d. per acre at Markwell in 1428, for example, 8d. per acre at Trelasker in 1447: P.R.O., C. 139/35, 139/126.
110. D.R.O., W 1258M/G/6/10; Arundell, M.A. 412; B.L. Add. roll 4658.
111. For example, D.C.A., V.C. 22279 (Sampford Courtenay), B.L. Add. roll 7658 (Hockford); D.R.O., C.R. 1132 (Monkleigh); D.R.O., W1258M/D/42/9 (Ottery in Lamerton).
112. P.R.O., S.C. 6/815/15 (Sampford Courtenay mill account); D.R.O., W1258M/D/52/2 (autumn ales). The reference to rye beer comes from outside the region, at Hele in Bradninch: S.R.O., DD. C.N. box 3 no. 14, account of 1372-3.
113. Fox, 'Farming techniques'; *Leland's Itinerary* (note 91), I, 224.
114. P.R.O., S.C. 61 815/15 for the year 1404. For such movements as seen through documents not of Duchy provenance, D.R.O. W1258M/D/52/2, account of 1479-80, P.R.O., S.C. 6/823/24, *Cal. Misc. Inq.*, V, 45 and D.R.O., C.R. 1132. For similar summering arrangements on Exmoor see Staffordshire Record Office, D. 593/A/1/14/4 and P.R.O., S.C. 6/826/21-3.
115. Fox, 'Farming techniques'.
116. D.R.O., W1258M/G/6/8; *Cal. Misc. Inq.*, V, 1.
117. D.R.O., W1258M/G/3; *Leland's Itinerary* (note 91), I, 172; *Cal. Misc. Inq.*, V, 45; P.R.O., S.C. 2/167/34 and D.R.O., W1258M/D/70, court of 1366 for redness.
118. Arundell, M.A. 236; see M. Kowaleski, 'Town and country in late medieval England: the example of the hide and leather trade' (unpublished paper, 1987).
119. Analysis of the poll tax returns for 1377 shows that population density in mid

Devon was particularly low: Fox, 'A study of field systems' (note 91), 67. Many of the parishes excused from taxation in 1428 because of small populations were in this region: *Feudal Aids*, I, 473-5.
120. J. Hare, 'Change and continuity in Wiltshire agriculture in the later middle ages', in W. Minchinton (ed.), *Agricultural Improvement: Medieval and Modern* (Exeter Papers in Economic History, 14, 1981), 18; J. Langdon, *Horses, Oxen and Technological Innovation* (1987), 275.
121. M.W. Beresford and H.P.R. Finberg, *English Medieval Boroughs: A Handlist* (1973), 48-9; Fox, 'Peasant farming'; E.M. Carus-Wilson, *The Expansion of Exeter at the Close of the Middle Ages* (University of Exeter, Harte Memorial Lecture, 1963).
122. J. Hatcher, 'A diversified economy: later medieval Cornwall', *Econ. Hist. Rev.*, 2nd ser., 22 (1969), 208-27; Fox, 'Peasant farming'.
123. H.S.A. Fox, 'The people of the wolds', (note 95).
124. Above Fig. 11, and Fox, 'Occupation of the land'.
125. M.M. Postan, 'Village livestock in the thirteenth century', *Econ. Hist. Rev.*, 2nd ser., 15 (1962), 247; C. Dyer, *Warwickshire Farming, 1349–c. 1520: Preparations for Agricultural Revolution* (Dugdale Society Occasional Papers, 27, 1981), 10.
126. The latest discussions are K. Biddick, 'Missing links: taxable wealth, markets and stratification among medieval English peasants', *J. Interdisciplinary History*, 18 (1987), 277-98 and B.M.S. Campbell, 'Agricultural progress in medieval England: some evidence from eastern Norfolk', *Econ. Hist. Rev.*, 2nd ser., 36 (1983), 37-40.
127. The environs of London may have been an exception, given the new estimates for the great size of that city in the thirteenth century. The new project on 'Feeding the City' at the Centre for Metropolitan History will help to clarify this point.

New towns for old? Reconstruction after fires in the South West: the case of Blandford Forum, Dorset, 1731.

by Michael Turner

A combination of flammable building materials and poor fire-fighting techniques in many pre-industrial towns could result in the rapid spread of accidental fires with losses of fifty, one hundred or more houses. Such occurrences were by no means rare, but they tend to be a neglected aspect of pre-industrial urban studies with the notable exception of one city—London—and one fire—that of 1666. Historians examining fires as part of the early modern urban experience generally ally them with other natural disasters—such as plague or the silting of harbours—which could lead to a town's economic and demographic collapse. Thus, fires are seen to precipitate the decline of small towns, or at best to inhibit change in those incapable of weathering the storm; the opportunities for improvements are only briefly acknowledged.[1] The compilation by E.L. Jones, S. Porter and M. Turner of *A Gazetteer of English Urban Fire Disasters, 1500-1900* now provides a foundation on which to build further research.[2] While the potential economic consequences of a major fire should not be underestimated, a study of over 500 provincial town fires listed in the *Gazetteer* suggests that few towns declined outright, while most were able to rebuild and maintain their position in the local economy.[3]

The ability of towns to rebuild is of considerable interest to historians concerned with urban renewal and contemporary attitudes to town planning and urban architecture. This paper outlines the susceptibility of south-western towns to major fires in the eighteenth century before examining the resulting potential for townscape change. Attention is focused on Blandford Forum, Dorset, which was largely destroyed in 1731. Blandford Forum illustrates both the difficulty of altering street patterns and the startling impact of post-fire buildings which resulted from minimum building regulations.

Blandford's renewed townscape is compared with other destroyed towns in the South West and some general conclusions are drawn regarding the perceptions and attitudes of contemporaries towards rebuilt towns.

I

The fire data compiled by Jones, Porter and Turner are of particular significance for the South West. Their *Gazetteer* records forty-two provincial town fires in eighteenth-century England which destroyed fifty or more houses. Thirteen of these fires occurred in Devon—principally including and to the east of Crediton—and extending into Dorset, which is a ratio of approximately one fire in these two counties to three elsewhere. Fires destroying a hundred or more houses display a similar ratio as seven out of twenty fires occurred in Devon and Dorset. The largest fires were in Crediton in 1743, (a loss of over 450 houses) followed by Blandford Forum (337 houses) and Tiverton (about 300 houses) which were destroyed on successive days in the summer of 1731. A concentration of fires in the South West is remarkable and did not go unnoticed at the time.[4] Thatch was used for roofing in many of the smaller south-western towns until well into the nineteenth century. It is highly combustible and efficient at spreading a fire when combined with a strong wind and, not unnaturally, this traditional building material was viewed as a principal cause of fires. Continued outbreaks throughout the eighteenth century led the London-based Phoenix Fire Office in 1807 to request other companies to join with them in increasing premiums:

> ... upon all thatched Buildings & their Contents in the Towns & Villages of Devonshire, Somersetshire & Dorsetshire, where the Generality of the Buildings are of that Description . . . as it is presumed the Experience of all the Offices has pretty fully established the necessity of a particular regulation for the Counties in Question, and as the Losses of this Company have invariably, for the last ten years, exceeded the Premiums received from these Counties.[5]

The other companies did not follow suit and it was not until the mid-nineteenth century that less flammable building materials such as slate and brick were adopted in sufficient quantity in the South West to act as fire breaks and curtail the size of subsequent fires. This change is doubtless connected with economic forces and a shift in taste; both were intimately associated with the spread of the railway into the South West which facilitated the import of new materials and ideas into the region.[6]

Demographic increase, economic prosperity, social and cultural change all contributed to the extent and nature of urban growth during the eighteenth century, but any development was primarily influenced by landownership and land availability. C.W. Chalklin's *Provincial Towns of Georgian England* is a most detailed study of the mechanics of the urban building process during this period.[7] Most of Chalklin's material is concerned with the development of sites and large urban estates. Town corporations were generally powerless to compel landlords to demolish and rebuild their properties, hence large-scale provincial urban development exemplified by Bristol or Bath was normally confined to green-field sites where new streets could be laid out subject only to the constraints of topography and the existing pattern of rural landownership. Not until the mid-eighteenth century did wider powers of compulsory purchase become available to a steadily increasing number of local town improvement commissions established by parliamentary acts to improve and redevelop town centres.[8] Urban fires destroyed existing properties which, in theory, provided an opportunity to regard the area as a green-field site and to plan new streets. This ideal was not fully implemented in London after 1666 as the multiplicity of individual tenures hindered large-scale replanning. However, some modifications to the street pattern were adopted—both in the capital and the provinces—by means of parliamentary rebuilding acts which conferred wide powers on a body of commissioners, for which London gave the lead.[9]

The impact of new buildings was invariably greater than that of street alterations. Towns experiencing major fires were by definition, composed of flammable building materials. Widespread destruction and the desire to prevent future fires encouraged builders to adopt brick and tile or slate. This change also facilitated the demise of traditional vernacular building in some towns in favour of a simplified urban classicism, now generally recognised as 'Georgian', which was more in keeping with current architectural taste. Thus, rebuilding could have profound consequences for the physical appearance of a destroyed town centre, but the social impact of new development also merits consideration. Peter Borsay identifies a post-Restoration renaissance of provincial urban culture. During this time Georgian terrace housing became the norm on the green-field urban sites documented by Mr. Chalklin.[10] New post-fire buildings also presented a Georgian face which constituted an immediate and obvious improvement which was unhesitatingly praised by contemporaries. Rebuilt towns could attract outsiders and there is also clear evidence that the county towns of Northampton and Warwick pursued a policy of encouraging wealthy newcomers—such as Justices of the Peace—to build and settle in the towns after their late seventeenth-century fires.[11] Blandford Forum did not enjoy the same county status as Northampton and Warwick, but nevertheless, its rebuilding was a model for towns in the South West.

II

Fire swept through the coaching and market town of Blandford Forum one June afternoon in 1731 (Fig. 14). It was apparently caused by sparks from a soap boiler's chimney landing on a thatched roof. The town's three hand-operated fire-engines were powerless to control the blaze and the engines themselves were abandoned after half an hour. Contemporaries noted that houses rebuilt with brick and tile after a small fire in 1713 at the end of East

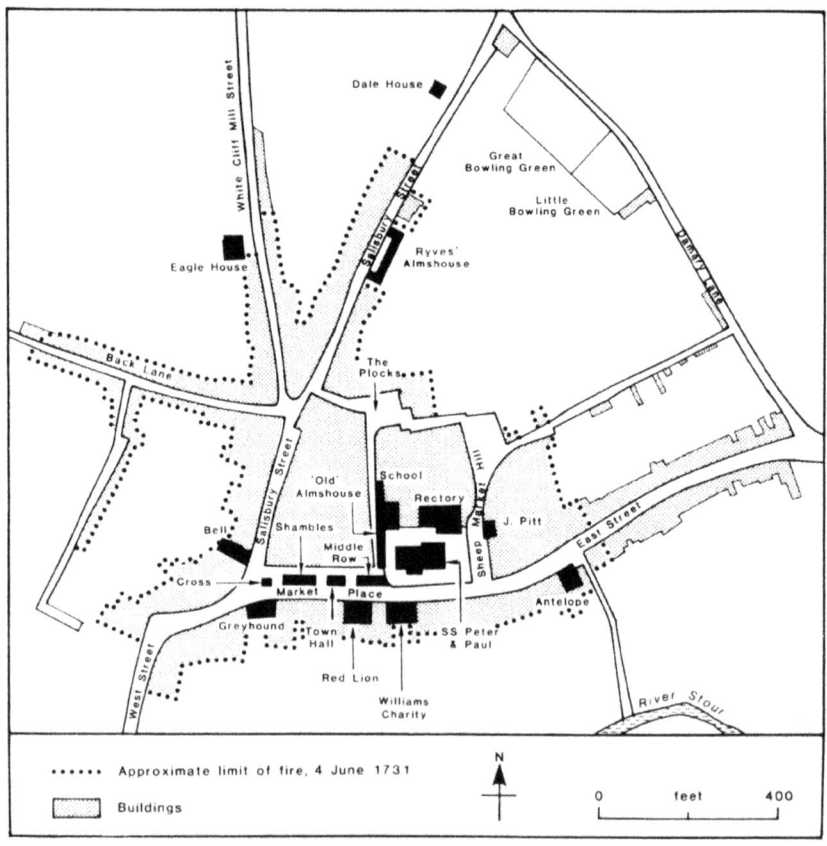

Fig. 14   Blandford Forum, c. 1731

Street escaped the second fire; this is clearly shown on an engraved map of the burnt town by John and William Bastard, local joiners and builder-architects.[12] The Bastard brothers also compiled a survey which included 337 destroyed dwelling houses, comprising some 80 per cent of the town, and they estimated the loss at over £44,000 in buildings and an additional £40,000 in goods.[13] An analysis of building materials recorded in their survey for over 500 buildings (including sheds and outhouses) reveals that 62 per cent of the destroyed properties were thatched. The survey confirms that thatch was a major factor in spreading the fire but its distribution in the town was uneven: tile dominated the prosperous centre and south-west of the town while the proportion of thatch increased with distance from the centre. The fire commenced in the White Cliff Mill Street area of the town where only 12 per cent of buildings were tiled, the remaining 88 per cent being covered with thatch. Conversely, 72 per cent of the buildings were tiled on the north side of the Market Place.[14] Even the high percentage of tile roofs in this area was insufficient to halt the rapidly spreading fire. This fact was clearly apparent to the inhabitants who subsequently sought to ban thatch on all new buildings (see below).

The inhabitants turned to securing food and temporary shelter immediately after the fire. Provisions were supplied by neighbouring towns and barracks were built for the homeless. Some finance was obtained from the Sun Fire Company, with which some householders were insured, and the sufferers also obtained a brief authorising collections on their behalf in neighbouring towns which eventually produced a distribution of a little over six shillings in the pound.[15] However, property disputes arose which obstructed rebuilding and this prompted the inhabitants to petition Parliament for assistance some eight months after the fire. The resulting Blandford Forum Rebuilding Act was modelled on legislation for London of 1667 which had previously been adapted for Northampton and Warwick after fires in 1675 and 1694 respectively.[16] The Act was titled *For the Better and more Easy Rebuilding* of Blandford Forum which indicates that both improvement and speed were envisaged and its clauses reflect contemporary expectation. Properties were to be rebuilt within four years or owners would risk compulsory purchase of their land. Rebuilding commissioners largely drawn from Dorset gentry were appointed to determine property disputes and to administer the act which included a ban on dangerous trades in the town centre. The act was also far-reaching in granting commissioners power to purchase land required for street widening and to enforce the use of lead, slate or tile for roofing throughout the town. The legacy of street alterations and new building left by the commissioners has affected the character of Blandford to this day.

Street alterations in Blandford were financed out of a £1,000 gift from

George II for public improvements, but the inertia caused by an established cadastre limited their extent. The commissioners restricted their activities to areas stated in the act and these mostly affected Corporation property or only a handful of individual owners. The pre-fire projection in Salisbury Street is shown on the Bastards' plan. The commissioners acted as arbitrators between the owners of the three properties concerned and the Corporation which compensated them. The result was the removal of three parcels of land totalling approximately a hundred feet long and a maximum of twenty feet deep. The commissioners were unable to create a straight line because one owner retained a seven-feet depth of land at the south end of this plot which resulted in a three-feet projection which remains today.[17] A building in East Street and two on the east side of Sheep Market Hill were altered in a similar way. More extensive changes took place on the west side of Sheep Market Hill which were designed to enlarge the churchyard of SS Peter and Paul (Fig. 15). The Corporation held the patronage of the church which was bordered by the rectory and a collection of Corporation-administered properties, including an almshouse and school. Public ownership of much of this extensive block of land facilitated alterations and the desired result was achieved by relocating buildings in a straight line to the north of the newly defined churchyard. A collection of small Corporation outbuildings was also relocated to straighten the west side of this street.[18]

A further improvement was achieved in the market place where three islands of buildings stood before the fire; owners were again compensated. The Middle Row was swept away and temporary shambles replaced formerly permanent structures. The town hall was rebuilt in 1734 on land to the north which was purchased out of the King's gift and the remains of the stone market cross to the west were dismantled the following year.[19]

Space precludes an extensive survey of post-fire properties in Blandford Forum, and reference should be made to volume three of the Royal Commission on Historical Monuments' inventory of Dorset for a more detailed examination of surviving buildings.[20] Architectural studies of Blandford justifiably concentrate on John and William Bastard whose public and private buildings still dominate the Market Place and form what Pevsner considered 'one of the most satisfying Georgian ensembles anywhere in England'.[21] The Bastards were both Blandford residents and the most influential of a number of architect-builders in the locality. The brothers held a high profile in the post-fire town and their map of the destruction and survey of losses have already been referred to. The Bastards were also significant figures in local government: both were members of the eleven-strong Corporation. John Bastard held the post of Borough Chamberlain from 1732 to 1736 and Bailiff from 1738 to 1740. William held the same posts in succession: in 1742–44

New towns for old? 81

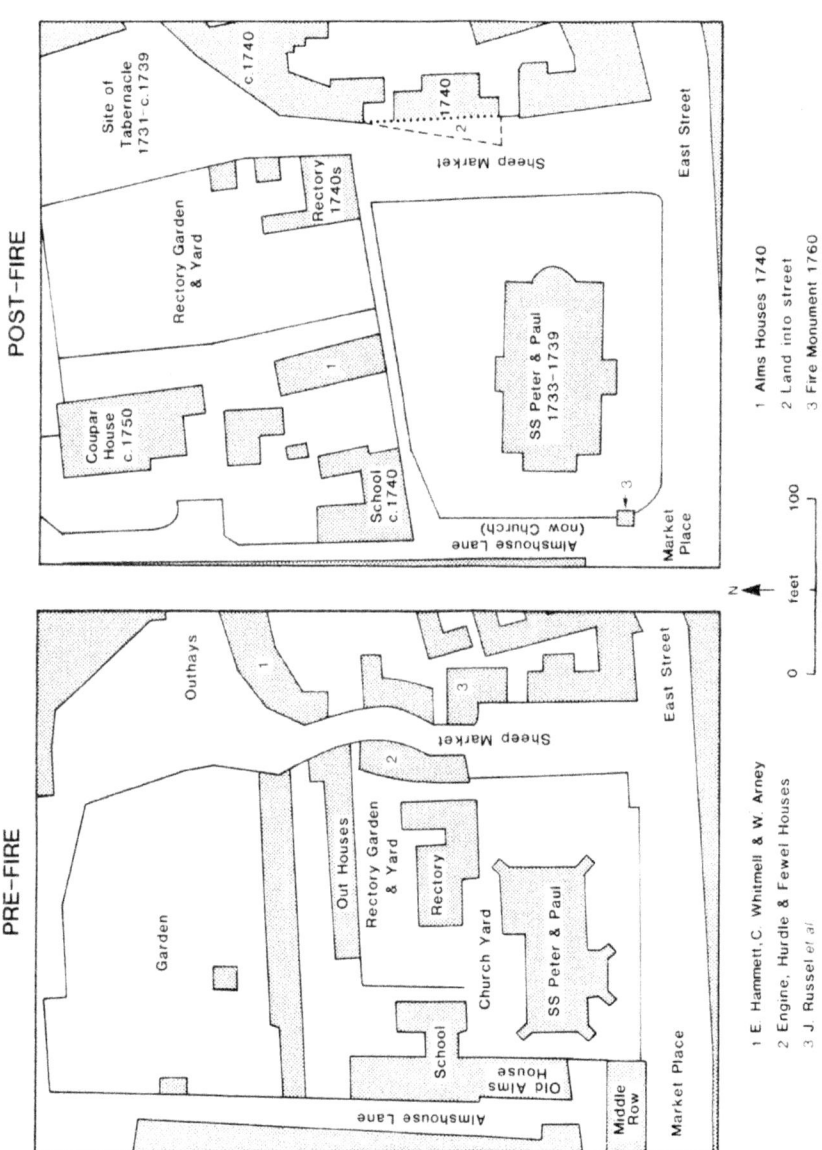

Fig. 15 Redevelopment of church and Sheep Market Hill, Blandford Forum, 1731–1760

and 1744-45 respectively, and he was also a Churchwarden in 1733-34.[22] The years 1732-36 formed a period of hectic building activity during which time the Bastards were working on major public buildings including the town hall and church. John Bastard controlled the Corporation's finances and, although there is no hint that he was guilty of corrupt practices as such, one of the perquisites of their offices was that Bastard & Co. were in a favourable position to secure these prestigious building contracts.

The stone-fronted town hall is an austere Palladian building on the north side of the market. It was designed by the Bastards, but is related to a sketch by Sir James Thornhill, one of the MPs for Weymouth and Melcombe Regis, and a rebuilding commissioner until his death in 1734.[23] The church to the east makes an even greater impact on account of its island site. It is the only known freestanding building by John and William and originally consisted of a simple apsed rectangle with classical dressings in marked contrast to the irregular plan of the former medieval church. The Bastards were also responsible for three large private buildings south of the market which were constructed in the 1730s according to fire insurance policies and their own testimony. These were the Greyhound Inn which they owned; the Red Lion, owned by a close relative; and the house they occupied on Williams' charity land which was administered by the Corporation.[24] All three buildings are three storeys high with applied classical orders and Baroque detailing which demonstrates the versatility of these provincial craftsmen. The seven-bay Greyhound is fronted with stucco while the other two are of red brick with darker vitrified bricks forming decorative panels. Both the Red Lion and their own house adopt a similar formula: a central carriageway with a lavish Baroque pedimented centrepiece above (Fig. 16).[25] Both also include Corinthian capitals with the well-known in-turned volutes favoured by a small school of Westcountry masons and builders.[26]

The fire signalled the end of the profusion of thatch and 'mudwall' or cob buildings recorded by the Bastards in their survey of losses. Much private post-fire rebuilding was more akin to the brick-built Eagle House in White Cliff Mill Street of c. 1730, or possibly the house of the glover George Elkins which was destroyed in the fire. Elkins' house stood on the south side of the market and was insured in 1730 for £300. The Bastards surveyed the remains of his stone, brick and tile dwelling in 1731, which formerly had two storeys plus an attic, and was the only house they described with sash windows. The Bastards valued it at thirty seven pounds per square (one hundred square feet) which is the highest value per square for any private property destroyed in the fire.[27] Blandford Forum was described by a traveller in 1735 as a 'large well new built town' by which time it had been transformed into a collection of contemporary buildings of a uniform character.[28] The design of

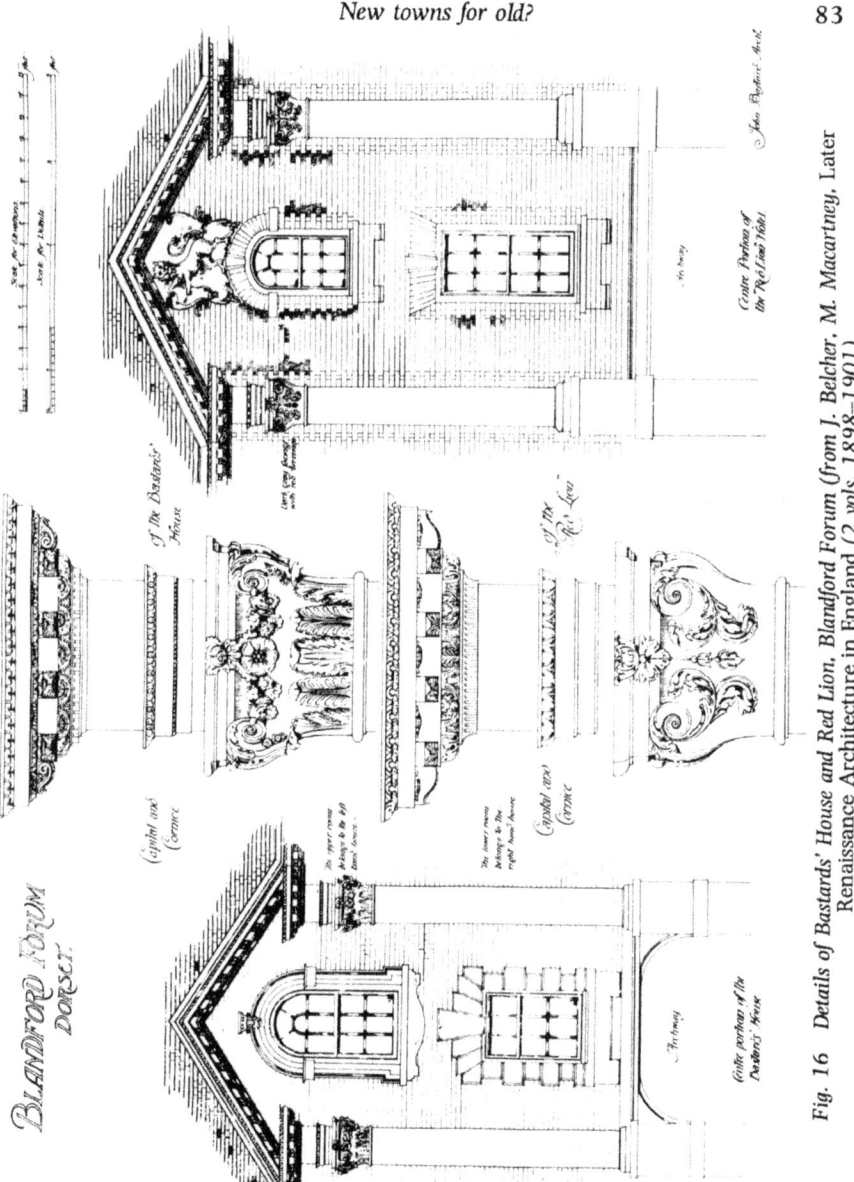

Fig. 16 Details of Bastards' House and Red Lion, Blandford Forum (from J. Belcher, M. Macartney, Later Renaissance Architecture in England (2 vols. 1898–1901)

private housing was not as adventurous as the Bastards' work, but much use was made of contrasting bricks for decorative effect. The use of brick and tile is confirmed by Sun Insurance policies taken out over an eighteen-month period between July 1732 and December 1733, the majority of which must relate to newly constructed buildings. Brick or stone walls are specified for sixty-five out of seventy-five buildings where the material is recorded, and tile for roofs is recorded in seventy-five out of ninety-three instances. There was strong pressure to refrain from using thatch which was banned by the act and the parish vestry was still enforcing this ruling in 1754.[29] Improvement was not limited to burnt properties. Eastway House and Lyston House are important post-fire brick buildings in East Street while Coupar House, of c. 1750, was constructed on land marked as a garden on the Bastards' map.[30]

Little is known, as yet, of the social impact of the rebuilding. Post-fire Blandford Forum was clearly expanding its function as a service centre for local gentry and Pococke observed the 'many good inns and shops' in 1754.[31] The Dorset historian John Hutchins noted 20 years later that:

> its chief support is the resort of travellers and the neighbouring gentry, its markets and fairs, and the races, which are commonly held ... in July and August, since the year 1729, and revived 1744.[32]

Town races held a significant position in the development of provincial culture and the list of attenders in 1786 is a testimony to their increasing popularity with the Dorset gentry.[33] The town patronised by travellers and county society in the mid-eighteenth century was in marked contrast to that of 1730 and it is fitting to conclude this discussion with the observation of one of the architects of that change: John Bastard. He built a classical monument in 1760 near the church to house a pump which is an unashamed expression of civic pride. The town was raised, states its inscription, 'like the PHAENIX from its ashes, to its present beautiful and flourishing state.'

III

There is little evidence of street plan alterations in other destroyed south-western towns during the eighteenth and early nineteenth centuries, with the exception of Wareham, Dorset and Chudleigh, Devon. A rebuilding act was obtained after the 1762 fire in Wareham (133 houses) and Chudleigh in 1807 (175 houses).[34] Once again, schemes were more likely to succeed where few landowners were involved and it is inferred that a determined body of people is required with the power to override individuals in the interests of improving the townscape. Modifications in Wareham and Chudleigh included some partial street widening and the removal of island buildings abutting their markets in a similar manner to alterations at Blandford Forum. Multiple landownership and the absence of committed co-ordinated action militated against similar schemes in other towns. A possible exception is Beaminster, Dorset, which was reputedly rebuilt with wider streets after a fire in 1684 destroyed seventy four houses, but this claim—which was made in 1914—is unsubstantiated.[35]

A change in building materials—often from traditional thatch to slate or tile—is more common than street plan alterations in most south-western towns. The Chudleigh fire prompted this almost overnight. West of England Fire Company insurance policies from January 1808 to March 1809 record fifty-three out of sixty-three properties as having slate, at least thirty-two of which can be identified as post-fire reconstructions.[36] Wareham's thatch dwellings were replaced with humble two-storey brick and tile houses which led Hutchins, who witnessed the rebuilding, to claim that the town 'rose fairer than before'.[37] It is difficult to assess objectively contemporary descriptions such as that of Read in 1746 who wrote of changes after Tiverton's 1731 fire for which a rebuilding act was also passed:

> The great Number of Gentlemen's Sons sent hither for their education is no small advantage to the town . . . and this, joined with the brisk trade carried here renders it so flourishing that, notwithstanding the dreadful calamity it underwent by fire in 1731, which almost totally consumed it, it is already elegantly rebuilt, and carries very few other marks of devastation other than the beauty of the new structures.[38]

Subsequent smaller fires in other parts of Tiverton did not significantly alter the effect of the 1731 fire and Dunsford later praised Tiverton as being the 'neatest inland town in Devon'. He recorded the prominence of red brick and slate houses except at the edge of the town and in areas which escaped the 'great fire'.[39]

The transformation possible after a fire, even without a rebuilding act, can be summarised with reference to Crediton, Devon. A detailed cadastral map illustrating the 1743 fire in West Town, Crediton, depicts a scattering of brick and slate houses inter-mixed with a majority of thatch and cob cottages with mullioned and transomed windows.[40] Andrew Brice described the town 16 years later:

> But now behold this demolish'd Part of the Town arisen (better than is pretended of the fabulous Phoenix) next to totally again out of its Ashes, with tenfold greater Beauty and Commodiousness; Numbers of Houses, on the Spot where stood old & low ones of but Mud, Daubing and Timber, being now erected high Brick, of a sort of Stucko, etc. etc. and many shining with Sash-Windows, & the like; in so much that one who had not seen the Place for nine or ten Years past, would scarce know this part to be *Crediton*.[41]

In spite of these changes, however, other parts of Crediton succumbed to repeated fires for another hundred years before sufficient adoption of fire-resistant materials and improved fire-fighting techniques contained subsequent outbreaks.[42]

IV

It is apparent that the example of Blandford Forum is not absolutely typical of rebuilding in the South West. Only Tiverton, Wareham and Chudleigh also obtained rebuilding acts and it is only in such towns that any evidence of street alterations is apparent. It is difficult to avoid the conclusion that large fires in the South West tended to prompt rebuilding acts which provided the necessary powers to enforce changes in landownership. A major exception is Crediton whose broad market street did not warrant alteration. But here, as elsewhere, building regulations were not necessary to raise the general standard of architecture, and in this respect Blandford Forum is only unique in the extent to which the achievement of a single building firm dominates its centre.

There is another aspect of rebuilding which also merits consideration. The title of this paper 'New towns for old?' is deliberately ambiguous. Eighteenth-century urban fires did not, of course, produce 'new towns' in the sense of pre-planned self-contained communities. If there are relatively few examples of re-planning, the buildings at least were new in more or less fashionable styles and building materials. It is tentatively suggested that rebuilding could not only alter contemporaries' perceptions of a town but also influence the extent of patronage by county society. English society in the eighteenth century is associated with a developing provincial urban culture and Read's comments on mid-eighteenth century Tiverton indicate that reconstruction and gentrification went hand in hand. He never addressed the question of which came first, but the fire either stimulated or reinforced an existing trend. In this context, Hutchins' reference to Dorset gentry frequenting Blandford Forum's revived races is tantalising in its brevity. Rebuilding begs the question to what extent could a fire prompt an upturn in a town's social status? The physical evidence of some post-fire reconstruction survives, but the contemporaries who enjoyed it do not. At present, not enough is known about who frequented these post-fire towns, nor how the pattern of landownership within the towns and suburbs was modified. However, rebuilding is clearly more than just a question of bricks and mortar and we await detailed local studies before we can adequately assess just how 'new' these 'new towns' really were.

Notes

1. J. Patten, *English Towns 1500-1700* (1978), 35, 60-65, 244-96 *passim*; P. Clark & P. Slack, *English Towns in Transition 1500-1700* (1976), 15, 99-100, 148-49. P. Corfield, *The Impact of English Towns 1700-1800* (1982), 175-76 briefly addresses improvement after fires in Warwick, 1694 and Blandford Forum, 1731.
2. E.L. Jones, S. Porter and M. Turner, *A Gazetteer of English Urban Fire Disasters 1500-1900* Historical Geography Research Series No.13 (1984).
3. An exception is Minehead, Somerset, but this was in decline before a fire in 1791 destroyed 72 houses and precipitated a temporary nadir in the town's fortunes. J. Savage, *History of the Hundred of Carhampton in the County of Somerset* (1830), 594, 652–53.
4. See J. Gilpin, *Western Tour* quoted in J. Hutchins, *The History and Antiquities of the County of Dorset* (3rd edn. 1861-73) vol. 1, 215; J. Dugdale, *The New British Traveller* (1819) vol. 2, 15.
5. Sun Fire Office General Committee Minute Book, 1798-1808, f.163; Guildhall Library, London, MS 11,931/8.
6. E.L. Jones, 'The reduction of fire damage in Southern England 1650-1850', *Post-Med. Arch.*, 2 (1968), 140-49; E.L. Jones, 'Fire disasters: the special case of East Devon', *Devon Historian*, 20 (1980), 11-17; S. Porter, 'Town fires: the case of Tiverton', *Dev. & Corn. N.Q.*, 33 (1977), 345-48.
7. C.W. Chalklin, *The Provincial Towns of Georgian England* (1974)
8. W. Ison, *The Georgian Buildings of Bath from 1700 to 1830* (1948); W. Ison, *The Georgian Buildings of Bristol* (1952); P. Clark (ed.), *Country Towns in Pre-industrial England* (1981), 21; E.L. Jones & M.E. Falkus, 'Urban improvement and the English economy in the seventeenth and eighteenth centuries' in P.J. Uselding (ed.), *Research in Econ. History*, 4 (1979), 214.
9. T.F. Reddaway, *The Rebuilding of London after the Great Fire* (1951 edn.). For post-fire improvements associated with rebuilding acts see M. Turner, 'The Nature of Urban Renewal after Fires in Seven English Provincial Towns, c. 1675-1810' (unpub. Ph.D. thesis, Exeter 1985).
10. P.N. Borsay, 'The English urban renaissance: the development of provincial urban culture c. 1680—c. 1760', *Social History*, 5 (1977), 581-603; P.N. Borsay, 'Culture, status and the English urban landscape', *History*, 67 (1982), 1-12; C.W. Chalklin 1974 (note 7).
11. M. Turner 1985 (note 9), 150-51; P. Styles, 'The Corporation of Warwick, 1660-1835', *Trans. Birmingham Arch. Soc.*, 59 (1938), 9-122. For JPs see A. Harding, *A Social History of English Law* (1966), 267-68.
12. R.C.H.M.(E.), *Dorset 3* (1970), plate 104.
13. J. Hutchins 1861-73 (note 4), vol. 1, 216-217; M. Blake, *A Brief Account of the Dreadful Fire at Blandford Forum ... 1731* (1735 edn.); J. Bastard 'Dimentions and valew of Buildings Lost & Detroi'd by Fire....', Dorset County Record Office, D6.
14. M. Turner 1985 (note 9), 45-47.
15. J. Hutchins 1861-73 (note 4), vol. 1, 217. For briefs see W.A. Bewes, *Church Briefs* (1896); C. Walford, 'King's briefs: their purposes and history', *Trans. Royal Hist. Soc.*, 10 (1882), 1-74.

16. 21 House of Commons Journals 811 (24 Feb. 1732); *An Act for the Better and More Easy Rebuilding of . . . Blandford*, 5 Geo. II c. 16 (1732). For Northampton and Warwick see M. Turner 1985 (note 9), *passim*.
17. J. Bastard (note 13); M. Turner 1985 (note 9), 232.
18. Cf R.C.H.M. (E.) 1970 (note 12) and Blandford Tithe Map, 1838, Dorset Record Office. Act for Rebuilding Blandford 1732 (note 16).
19. M. Turner 1985 (note 9), 232-33.
20. R.C.H.M.(E.) 1970 (note 12), 16-40.
21. N. Pevsner & J. Newman, *Dorset* (1972), 95; H.M. Colvin, 'The Bastards of Blandford', *Arch. J.*, 104 (1947), 178-95; J. Adams 'Bastards of Blandford', *Architectural Rev.*, 143 (1968), 445-50.
22. M. Turner 1985 (note 9), 286-87.
23. H.M. Colvin 1947 (note 21), 186; H.M. Colvin, *A Biographical Dictionary of British Architects 1600-1840* (1978), 824-26.
24. J. Bastard (note 13), 19-20; J. Hutchins 1861-73 (note 4), vol.3, 523.
25. Fig. 16 is taken from J. Belcher & M. Macartney, *Later Renaissance Architecture in England*, vol. 1 (1898), plate 81.
26. This feature reflects the influence of Thomas Archer (1668-1743) and ultimately derives from Borromini, see J. Adams 1968 (note 21); H.M. Colvin 1978 (note 23), 68-70.
27. The two highest value properties per square were the Town Hall (£40) and Church (£50), J. Bastard (note 13); R.C.H.M.(E.) 1970 (note 12), 27-28. For the 'square' see R. Neve, *The City and Country Purchaser* (1969 edn.), 243.
28. B. L., Add. MS. 5957, f.18.
29. Sun Fire Office Policy Registers, Old Series vols. 34-37, Guildhall Library, London, MS 11,936; SS. Peter & Paul, Blandford Forum, Vestry Book, 20 May 1754, Dorset County Record Office, P70/VE1.
30. For descriptions of these houses see R.C.H.M.(E.) 1970 (note 12), 24-25, 29-30.
31. R. Pococke, *The Travels Through England*, Camden Soc. 2 (1889), 140-41.
32. J. Hutchins, *The History and Antiquities of the County of Dorset*, Vol.1 (1774), 75.
33. J. Hutchins 1861-73 (note 4), vol. 1, 215-216. For Warwick races see P.N.Borsay 1977 (note 10), 583.
34. *Act for Rebuilding Wareham*, 3 Geo. III c. 54 (1762); *Act for Rebuilding Chudleigh*, 48 Geo. III c. lxxxix (local & personal, 1808).
35. R. Hine, *History of Beaminster* (1914), 123-26.
36. West of England Fire Company Agent's Policy Register 1, 1808-1809, and Policy Register A, 1808-1816, Commercial Union Assurance, Exeter; F. Corfield, *Chudleigh Fire* (1808). For post-fire adoption of slate, see T.H. Williams, *The Environs of Exeter* (1815) n.p.
37. J. Hutchins 1861-73 (note 4), vol.1, 81.
38. T. Read, *The English Traveller*, vol.1, (1746), 287.
39. M. Dunsford, *Historical Memoirs of the Town and Parish of Tiverton* (1790), 295-96.
40. Plan of Crediton, c. 1743, D.R.O., 2065 Madd.3.
41. A. Brice, *The Grand Gazetteer, or Topographic Dictionary* (1759), 387.
42. T.W. Venn, 'History of Crediton' vol. 2 (3rd revision, 1961), 99, deposited in Exeter Westcountry Studies Library.

Acknowledgements

Part of the research on which this paper is based was funded by a Social Science Research Council award (1978-81) under the supervision of Dr. R.J.P. Kain, Exeter University. Dr. S. Porter kindly commented on the text, and I am also grateful to Gill Alexander, Queen's University, Belfast, for figs. 14 and 15, and Andrew Teed, Exeter University, for photographing fig. 16.

The Georgian landscape garden: Devon in the national context.

by Steven Pugsley

The true born Devonian, it has been said, is loathe to own that his native county will admit of any improvement whatsoever. Such a sentiment notwithstanding, the landscape of Devon is largely the product of the effort of man, usually for his profit, sometimes for his pleasure. The county's comparatively remote situation never isolated it entirely from the spirit of agricultural improvement nor from prevailing fashions for the treatment of amenity land. Certainly from the age of George I to the time of George IV many of its rolling acres were subjected to that taste which sought to produce pleasure grounds that imitated, and integrated with, nature rather than dominated or stood divorced from it: landscape gardening.

Devon's farming practices were reasonably advanced in the late seventeenth century, and by 1700 a high proportion of the county had been enclosed.[1] Risdon, as early as the 1630s, remarked that landowners were willing to sacrifice their parks—and thus, presumably, their deer hunting—by disparking and turning from 'pasturing wild beasts to the breeding and feeding of cattle, sheep and tillage'.[2] Enclosure, coupled with the county's undulating topography, served to inhibit the development in Devon of the full-blown French-inspired baroque garden, which had appeared in England during the reign of Charles II. This mode of garden design required a relatively flat surface for its geometric parterres (that is, patterned beds of flowers) and ornamental bodies of water, and wide expanses of open countryside for the planting of avenues of trees. It is surely significant, bearing in mind the matter of terrain, that Jan Kip and Leonard Knyff did not include a single engraving of a Devon garden in their book of views of country seats, entitled *Britannia Illustrata*, published in 1708.[3]

Devon's gardens at the beginning of the eighteenth century seem to have been on a comparatively small scale, but none the less to have exhibited features common to the national showpieces in which Knyff and Kip specialized. Their appearance is best conveyed in the collection of drawings produced by the amateur topographer Edmund Prideaux.[4] Visiting relatives and friends in 1716 and 1727 he executed a series of sketches of their houses and estates. These range from Soldon, near Holsworthy, with its small parterre, simple rectangles of grass and a few decorative trees; to Dunsland in Bradford parish, with small, walled enclosures reminiscent of the introspective medieval garden, but with straight rides cut through the adjoining woods; to Forde Abbey which possessed by far the grandest garden Prideaux depicted in Devon (Fig. 17).

At Forde the panoply of clipped evergreens, formal cascade and canal, and radiating avenues of trees, are a near perfect expression of the French school of gardening. Cartesian philosophy had offered the vision of human mastery of nature. The Frenchman André Le Nôtre (1613-1700) strove to give gardening form to this ideal at Versailles and elsewhere. By clipping trees into extraordinary shapes, torturing the ground with symmetrical embroideries, harnessing the powers of water and planting avenues of trees stretching out to the far horizon, he demonstrated man's complete control of nature and, by implication, Louis XIV's total domination of his country. The later Stuarts, in their envy or their desire to emulate French absolutism established it as the court gardening style and this percolated down even to the level of the Soldon parterre.

Marlborough's wars, and the defeat of France had, however, considerably reduced the stock of the French and their culture in the eyes of the English, who became correspondingly more patriotic and self-confident. They were less inclined to respect—in the words of the 3rd Earl of Shaftsbury—the 'Mockery of Princely Gardens' (Versailles foremost amongst them).[5] The antithesis of such artifice was unspoiled nature in its primitive state which could, in turn, be equated with the great English virtues of liberty and freedom. With the decline of French influence on garden design, attention was turned instead to precedents drawn from classical antiquity, venerated by the classically educated English as the golden age of human achievement. Classical literature provided the model of an idealized nature in Arcadia, and hints of the partial informality of Roman gardens. Moreover, the enticing and much sought-after pictures of Salvator Rosa and Caspar Dughet had—along with the grand tour—made familiar the Roman landscape and heightened the desire to recreate on northern shores aspects of the Campagna. It would be a mistake, though, to assume that these new concepts and ideals produced at once the kind of total landscape that we would associate with Capability Brown later in the century. Instead, the 1730s and 40s were a transitional phase in which elements of formality and natural gardening existed side by side.

The Georgian landscape garden

Fig. 17 Forde Abbey, Thorncombe (now Dorset). The French-inspired formal garden, as depicted by Edmund Prideaux in c. 1727

Prideaux, no later than 1727, had shown a parterre with statues and topiary adjoining the house at Heanton Satchville. By 1739, when a view of Heanton was published in Badeslade and Rocque's *Vitruvius Britannicus*, this had been levelled and replaced with a smooth lawn; considerably smaller formal gardens were still in existence, but at some distance from the house.[6] At Mount Edgcumbe, across the water from Plymouth, Badeslade clearly indicates a succession of formal ponds to the west of the house and an area of geometrical planting in the formal manner to the east (Fig. 18). In the foreground, however, a so called 'wilderness' of trees can be observed, highly irregular in pattern.[7] This layout does not appear in Prideaux's drawings of Mount Edgcumbe, and so most probably belongs to the 1730s. It is therefore contemporary with one of the most outstanding transitional gardens at Lord Burlington's Chiswick, although the latter is undeniably more extensive, better populated with classical buildings to remind one of the ancients (Mount Edgcumbe has just one temple in the midst of the Wilderness) and with paths decidedly more sinuous and thus 'natural'.[8]

The full influence of Chiswick and its kindred landscapes at Claremont and Stowe becomes fully apparent in the *c.* 1730s design for Boringdon at Plympton, then the home of John Parker.[9] Similarities between the disposition of the groves at both Boringdon and Chiswick are marked. The anonymous designer probably had access to Rocque's engraving of the Chiswick plan, although the local example of Mount Edgcumbe might have been an equally potent inspiration. More certainly, the projected Temple of the Worthies and the Altar of the Saxon Gods are derived from the Temple of the British Worthies and the Altar of the Saxon Gods at Stowe in Buckinghamshire. These were designed by Burlington's protégé William Kent, who had trained as a painter and, at least partly as a consequence, tended to envisage his garden settings as though in an Italian painting. And clearly Boringdon was—like a portion of Stowe—to have been a pictorially based garden of association in which the ideas and sensations provoked by an object or scene were as important as their purely visual qualities: in the case of the Temple and of the Altar (by analogy with Stowe) thoughts of the founders and defenders of British liberty and by implication the patriotic foundations of the new gardening style.

The type of softened formality practiced by Kent's occasional colleague Bridgeman was also finding favour in Devon at this time. Bicton, *c.* 1735, is sometimes attributed to Le Nôtre, although a trifle implausibly as by this date he had been dead for thirty-five years. Nevertheless, the notion of a prolonged axis across a valley is French, and was used by Le Nôtre at Vaux-le-Vicomte and Versailles. But Bridgeman, equally, was fond of the long avenue culminating in an eye catcher such as one finds at Bicton and, though no

The Georgian landscape garden

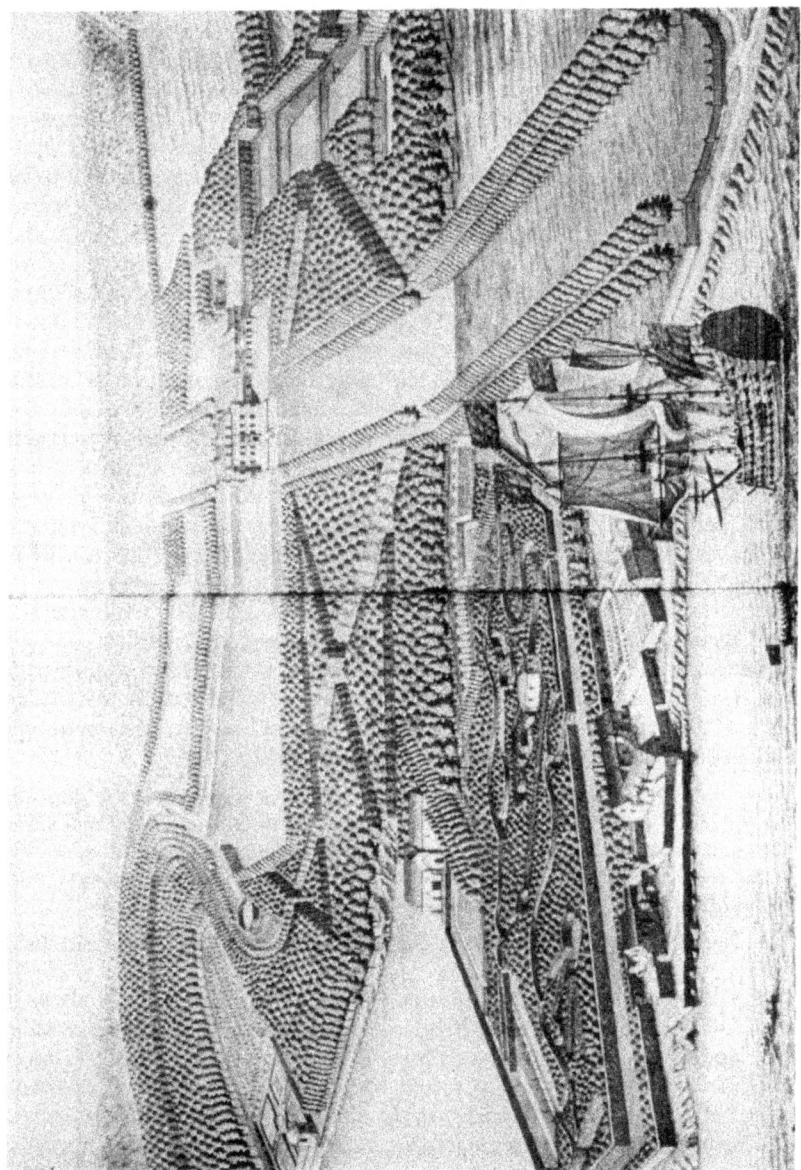

Fig. 18   Mount Edgcumbe, Cremyll (now Cornwall). Drawn and engraved by Badeslade and Rocque. c. 1739 (From: Vitruvius Britannicus, Vol. iv, 1739)

designer is known to have been responsible for the garden, the grass terraces leading to a regular body of water are Bridgemanesque devices.[10]

Bicton is remarkably similar in plan to Castle Hill, Filleigh, although Castle Hill is perhaps a little earlier, as work on rebuilding the house was commenced in 1729 (Fig. 19).[11] Lord Clinton, the master of Castle Hill, was a frequent visitor to France according to Horace Walpole, and undoubtedly when his brother remodelled the gardens later in the century they were thought to be in the 'false French Taste'.[12] On the other hand, Lord Burlington acted as an architectural adviser to Clinton in the reconstruction of the mansion, and might be expected to have favoured something in the Kentian manner. In truth, Castle Hill is typical of this transitional phase in that it exhibited more than one style of gardening. As at Bicton, a series of grass terraces led down from one side of a valley to a symmetrical pond, with a straight avenue ascending on the opposite side with an eye catcher (an arch) at its zenith. But the numerous garden buildings, real or imaginary, which are scattered through the landscape in the 1741 paintings of Castle Hill by Lange[13] suggest an intent of pictorial association, similar to that of Clinton's brother-in-law George Lyttleton, at Hagley in Worcestershire. Indeed, the sham Castle on the hill behind the house and from which it takes its name is probably contemporary with Sanderson Miller's much more famous gothic ruin (of c. 1747-8) at Hagley, and some interchange of ideas is to be suspected.

Before his death in 1751 Lord Clinton began to consider removing the formal elements of the Castle Hill landscape. In the event this task was left to his brother Matthew, the 2nd Baron Fortescue, in the 1770s, acting with advice from his steward Hilliard. Care was taken none the less not to sacrifice aspects of the existing scheme merely for the sake of the then predominating fashion. As Hilliard wrote to Fortescue in June 1771:

> Your Lordship's idea of planting clumps to take off the formality of the slopes in the paddock may have a pleasing effect ... (but) the rectilineal form of that scene though it may not please the casual spectator, yet when considered as an outline to the necessary regularity of the house and platform has some propriety in it though not comfortable to the present taste.[14]

The formal urge was evidently deeply rooted, and the slopes, in fact, survived relatively unscathed.

It should be emphasised that in none of the Devon gardens noted above is any professional designer known to have been at work. Rather, the inspiration of the landowning patron himself probably accounts for the layout in most cases. Nor was this situation unusual elsewhere in the country: Painshill (Surrey), Hagley, The Leasowes (Shropshire) and Stourhead (Wiltshire), some of the most renowned mid eighteenth century landscapes, were all created

The Georgian landscape garden

Fig. 19 Castle Hill, Filleigh. The transitional landscape, from a painting by Jo. Lange, 1741

by amateurs. This spirit of idiosyncratic improvement lived on throughout the century. Fortescue, with Hilliard, at Castle Hill, apparently relied merely on the printed work of Batty Langley and counsel from friends and relations. Mount Edgcumbe was turned into one of the most visited landscapes in England under the guidance of the 1st and 2nd Earls of Mount Edgcumbe from 1761; they exploited its natural setting to produce a series of contrasts between enclosed gardens and glades, and wide vistas over land and sea, which in turn were intended to excite a series of different emotions from the visitor—of gloom and delight, ecstacy and fear.[15] At Oxton, Kenn, the Rev. John Swete began in 1781 to remodel the garden, which he found to be:

> environed by garden walks, by an artificial terrace where old yews form'd an avenue of Pyramids, by orchards and intersecting hedges . . .

and which he transformed into

> a sweet valley . . . gently descending between old woods of oak, through which a rivulet crept on . . .[16]

Beside the continuance of individual effort must, however, be set the rise of the professional landscape gardener from around 1750, a phenomenon not unconnected with the advance of the professional architect. Foremost amongst them was Lancelot Brown, usually known by the nickname 'Capability'. Brown endeavoured, primarily, to create a perfect state of nature, eliminating 'false accidents' and in this way returning it to the simplicity that existed in the ancient world (such a drive for first principles being characteristic of the neo-classicism of the later 18th century). To this end the emblems and ornaments of the associational garden were dispensed with, and the landscape filled with three simple representative elements: wood, water and grass. Having discovered a formula in the 1740s that utilized them suc- cessfully, he repeated it with little variation in his remodelling of a high proportion of English seats. In simple terms, this consisted of a perimeter belt of woodland encircling a park of gentle hills, within which were placed clumps of trees and a sheet of water in the middle distance from the house; the park was allowed to run right up to the residence effectively removing its foreground.

Brown's earliest work in Devon is thought to have been at Widdicombe House, Stokenham in the 1750s, where his client was a Holdsworth of the Dartmouth family. Very little survives of his putative plantations apart, perhaps, from the remnants of a timber belt, and nothing whatsoever of the pineapple house and lawns which he reputedly designed.[17] Nor is Sharpham at Totnes anything other than a landscape attributed to Brown by traditon.[18] At Ugbrooke, Chudleigh, on the other hand, the evidence of Brown's involvement is clear in the park he laid out for the 4th Baron Clifford around 1770 (Fig. 20). In many respects it is characteristic, although more rugged than most: perimeter planting running along the horizon, with parkland sweeping down to groups of trees, the lake and then right up to the house itself.[19] Such were its beauties that the Clifford's chaplain, Father Joseph Reeve, was driven to compose a poem, published in 1776, entitled *Ugbrooke Park*, wherein he wrote:

> Hence thro' the whole irregularly great,
> Nature and Art the wond'rous work complete;
> In all so true, so unperceived the skill,
> That Nature modified is Nature still.[20]

Brown's last foray into the county came in 1773 when the 3rd Viscount Lisburne sought his advice about the repair of Mamhead House and the improvement of its grounds. No water seems to have been introduced into the landscape (the sea, after all, is clearly visible from the estate) but correspondence from Lord Lisburne indicates that Brown's directions for planting were followed.[21]

The Brownian manner was not unique to Brown, however, and during his lifetime and after his death in 1783, many sought to work within the parameters of landscape design which he had established. Of these one might mention Richmond, who had a small practice in the south of England, and who in 1769 was introduced to the Parkers at Saltram by their friends the Pelhams of Stanmer in Sussex. Richmond was apparently capable of designing buildings as well as planting schemes, for in 1773 Theresa Parker described the orangery as 'Stockman's improvements upon a plan he saw of Mr. Richmond's'.[22] The agriculturalist turned ornamental improver, William Marshall, visited Buckland Abbey in 1791 and urged Sir Francis Henry Drake to cut back overgrown woods into decent masses in order to render the air more wholesome whilst at the same time revealing the undulations of the ground.[23] And, perhaps most celebrated of all in Devon, John Veitch, son of an Edinburgh nurseryman, came to Killerton in 1771 at the bidding of Sir Thomas Acland, the 7th baronet, and proceeded to lay out the park of 500 acres.[24] Killerton seems to have become his primary concern, but he established a wider reputation as a nurseryman and landscape designer, contracting for the making of roads and the planting of trees at Shute in the early 1790s, for example.[25]

The mantle of Brown fell most easily onto the shoulders of Humphry Repton. Having decided almost upon a whim to become a landscape gardener in 1788, he garnered nearly two hundred commissions before 1816.[26] By and large Repton followed Brown's precepts, although he favoured lusher

100 *Landscape and Townscape in the South West*

Fig. 20 Ugbrooke, Chudleigh. The 'natural' park laid out for the 4th Baron Clifford by 'Capability' Brown, around 1770

planting, moving water rather than a lake, and—highly importantly—recommended the use of a terrace or balustraded walk and occasional flower beds to act as an area of transition between the park and the house. In Devon his two landscapes were designed to surround newly erected houses. The first in 1799 was for the banker Charles Hoare at Luscombe Castle, Dawlish.[27] Tellingly, in his customary Red Book of designs for the property, he advocated 'an adequate foreground of highly dressed Lawn and Pleasure Garden on which trees may be planted to vary the surface . . .' and so provide sources of 'cheerfulness and intricacy'.[28] Variety and intricacy: the very qualities central to the late eighteenth-century Picturesque movement, and whose absence from a Brown park was held to be so regrettable by the Picturesque theorists Richard Payne Knight and Uvedale Price. In their regard for a landscape of contrasts of light and shade, and subtleties of texture and colouring such as only a painter could conceive, they raised the fundamentally early eighteenth-century concept to its highest pitch. Repton was too practical a man to subscribe fully to the wilder excesses of Picturesque theory—for instance, that a mouldering ruin was, in visual terms, to be preferred to a well kept dwelling—but he none the less adhered to some of its principles. This is obvious at Endsleigh, Milton Abbot, where Jeffry Wyatville had built a sprawling Cottage Ornée for the 6th Duke of Bedford in 1810-11.[29] Like Luscombe, the house is full of intricacy and variety and this was echoed in the gardens that Repton provided immediately around the house as part of his scheme of 1814; this included a children's flower garden and a terrace with a conservatory, rock plants and fruit walls (Fig. 21).[30]

Part of the reason, of course, for this increased interest in flowers and plants were the growing numbers of new introductions from throughout the world. After 1800, 150 new varieties a year were brought to England.[31] Intricacy and variety, which in the garden at Fordlands, Ide, as delineated by T.H. Williams in 1815,[32] were expressed by rustic temples and seats, began to be signified instead by a kaleidoscopic array of exotics. As Barbara Jones has said, the focus had changed, 'the eye looking close instead of across the valley, not at a plantation but a rose'.[33] This development is exemplified by Knowle Cottage, Sidmouth, which came into the possession of the Fish family in the 1820s and by 1836, when it was described by *Mockett's Journal*, contained orange and lemon trees 'together with many other superior and rare plants which excite the admiration of all florists'. A park of sorts it had, but stuffed with rare animals like a zoo and obviously of less moment than the flower garden.[34]

Growing the plants of warmer climes demanded the control of nature, aided by the new technology of the industrial revolution. The Palm House at Bicton, erected at some time between 1818 and 1838 is a pioneering example of

Fig. 21 Endsleigh, Milton Abbot. The picturesque landscape seen from the house, as envisaged by Humphry Repton. (From: Fragments on the Theory and Practise of Landscape Gardening, 1816)

iron and glass construction.[35] It contained within it what was effectively a landscape of itself. Thus, it symbolizes the end of the free reign of nature and of the landscape garden, and confidently marks the dawn of the age of the flower gardener and the specialised plant collector.

Notes

1. See M.A. Havinden, 'Agricultural history in the South West', and R. Stanes, 'Devon agriculture in the mid 18th-Century: the evidence of the Milles enquiries', in M.A. Havinden and C.M. King (eds.), *The South West and the Land* (1969).
2. T. Risdon, *Survey of the County of Devon* (1810 edn.), 6-7.
3. L. Knyff and J.Kip, *Britannia Illustrata* (1707).
4. The Prideaux drawings, edited by John Harris, are reproduced in *Architectural History*, 7 (1964).
5. Anthony Ashley Cooper, 3rd Earl of Shaftesbury, *The Moralists* (1709).
6. T. Badeslade and J. Rocque, *Vitruvius Britannicus*, Vol IV (1739), plates 73-74.
7. Badeslade and Rocque, *ibid*, plates 94-95.
8. Badeslade and Rocque, *ibid*, plates 82-83.
9. Discussed by J. Cornforth, 'The Making of Saltram Landscape' *C(ountry) L(ife)*, 142, (1967), 594-595. The Boringdon plan, currently in the RIBA collection, is reproduced.
10. For Bridgeman, see P. Willis, *Charles Bridgeman and the English Landscape Garden* (1977).
11. For Castle Hill generally, see K. Woodbridge, 'Landscaping at Castle Hill', *C.L.*, 165 (1979), 18-21; R. Fausset, 'The Creation of the Gardens at Castle Hill', *Garden History*, 13, No.2 (1985), 102-125; *ibid*, 15, No.2 (1987), 167-171; and Hugh, 4th Earl Fortescue, *A Chronicle of Castle Hill* (1929). I am indebted to Lady Margaret Fortescue for many invaluable discussions concerning this remarkable landscape.
12. D.R.O., 1262M/ E29-18. Fortescue to Hilliard. n.d. c. 1771.
13. Reproduced in *C.L.*, 75 (1934), 275, and J. Harris, *The Artist and the Country House* (1979), Nos. 186 and 186b.
14. D.R.O., 1262M/ E29-17. Hilliard to Fortescue. 23rd June, 1771.
15. See M. Girouard and Baron Porcelli, 'Mount Edgcumbe', *C.L.*, 128 (1960), 1550-1553, 1598-1601.
16. D.R.O., 564/M. F2. J. Swete, *Devon Tour*, Vol 2 (1792), 1-6.
17. I am grateful to Mrs. J.Breach for information concerning Widdicombe. See also D. Stroud, *Capability Brown* (new edn 1975), 244 and R. Turner, *Capability Brown* (1985), 187.
18. D. Stroud, 1975, 238, and R. Turner, 1985, 192. (see note 17).
19. A. Rowan, 'The Landscape at Ugbrooke, Devon' *C.L.*, 142 (1967), 790-793.
20. J. Reeve, *Ugbrooke Park—A Poem* (1776), lines 353-356.
21. D. Stroud, 1975, 97-98. (see note 17).
22. J. Cornforth, 'The Making of the Saltram Landscape', *C.L.*, 142 (1967), 594-597.
23. W. Marshall, *Planting and Rural Ornament*, Vol I (1796), 376-379.

24. A. Acland, *A Devon Family* (1981), chapters 3 and 6.
25. Pole-Carew Papers. PE/30/32 (Antony House).
26. For Repton, see D. Stroud, *Humphry Repton* (1962) and C. Carter, P. Goode and K. Laurie (eds), *Humphry Repton Landscape Gardener* (1982).
27. C. Hussey, 'Luscombe Castle, Devon' *C.L.*, 119 (1956), 248-251, 292-295, 336-339.
28. Quoted by C. Hussey, *English Country Houses: Late Georgian* (1958), 60.
29. C. Hussey, 'Endsleigh, Devon' *C.L.*, 130 (1961), 246-249, 296-299.
30. H. Repton, *Fragments on the Theory and Practise of Landscape Gardening* (1816), Fragment xxxiv, 213-226.
31. D.C. Stuart, *Georgian Gardens* (1979), 105, points out that the Loddiges by *c*.1820, could list nearly a quarter of the world's then known flora in their nursery catalogue.
32. T.H. Williams, *The Environs of Exeter*, Part I (1815).
33. B. Jones, *Follies and Grottoes* (2nd ed. 1974), 250.
34. *Mockett's Journal* (1836). For Knowle Cottage, see also J. Harvey, *Guide to Knowle Cottage, Sidmouth* (1834); S.F. Hoyte (pub.), *A Guide to Knowle Cottage, Sidmouth, the Villa of T.L. Fish* (n.d.);—*New Guide to Knowle Cottage, Sidmouth* (1840).
35. S. Koppelkamm, (trans. K. Talbot), *Glasshouses and Wintergardens of the Nineteenth Century* (1981), .55.

The reform of urban management and the shaping of Plymouth's mid-Victorian landscape

by Mark Brayshay

In considering the development of the Victorian urban landscape, the popular view would probably be that there is little evidence of conscious planning or effective management before the last quarter of the nineteenth century when the famous 1875 *Public Health Act*, passed during Disraeli's second administration, enabled municipal authorities to frame bye-laws controlling building standards, sanitary installations and other environmental amenities.[1] Indeed, the term laissez-faire is so frequently used in conjunction with the development of towns in the early Victorian period that our attention has been diverted away from precisely how much environmental management and control was actually being exercised in certain towns in the years before 1875. Of course, the philosophy of laissez-faire and self-help was so much a part of the Victorian ethos, that it is perhaps no surprise that some historians have believed that, despite the evidence of an increasingly collectivist and interventionist approach to the management of our towns, development was somehow still largely conforming to the ideology of non-interference. But Derek Fraser has argued that from the time of the *Municipal Corporations Act* of 1835, through until the 1880s and 1890s, a gradual, though sweeping, revolution occurred in the manner of government of English towns.[2] He suggests, moreover, that although there was never a theory of collectivism to rival the entrenched philosophy of laissez-faire, collectivism nonetheless *evolved* out of the purely pragmatic response of Victorian local government to urban social problems. As steps were taken to tackle practical borough problems, local authorities thus became ever more deeply committed to interventionist policies. By the end of the nineteenth century, town councils were assuming extraordinarily wide responsibility for the general welfare of the community. And this broadening definition of their social purpose in fact originated fifty years earlier in a commitment to public health and environmental management. Thus, while in early Victorian England the creation of a 'wholesome' environment was seen principally in terms of sanitary regulation, by later Victorian times, it was seen as supplying a wide range of cultural and recreational needs as well.[3]

The commitment of late Victorian borough authorities to the promotion of a healthy and well-served environment led ultimately towards the next logical step—the idea of town planning.[4] Arguably, therefore, although town planning legislation was not enacted until the present century, its roots stretch deep into Victorian times, and although few self-respecting Victorian town councillors would consciously acknowledge a philosophical or ideological commitment to collectivism, paradoxically the practical evidence of municipal activity, glimpses of which survive in today's townscapes, resulted directly from interventionist policies.

Perhaps because of a long allegiance on the part of social and political historians to the notion of laissez-faire in Victorian towns, and perhaps also because the landscape impact of early interventionist policies may seem somewhat modest in scale when compared with the very obviously planned townscapes of modern times, very little attention has been paid to the direct role of municipal authorities in shaping the development of our towns and cities in the period before 1900, and certainly before 1875. The argument that provincial town councils and other local bodies neither possessed nor wanted the power to influence the kind of development which occurred within their boundaries has been too readily accepted. Although it would be false to claim steady and uniform progress towards widespread interventionist urban management, certain towns were remarkably innovative. Much depended, of course, upon the varying levels of local prosperity and the scale of urban expansion.[5] Growth, after all, tended not only to exacerbate environmental problems, but also swelled local rates revenue, thereby offering funds which could be applied to secure solutions. Permissive legislation and a politically progressive ruling party were further crucial ingredients in the local equation, which helps to explain why some Victorian towns came to be more actively and decisively managed than others.[6] Thus, in a rapidly expanding town like mid-Victorian Plymouth, enjoying a substantial increase in wealth and prosperity, and ruled for a long period by a radical, liberal elite, the terms of the enabling measures enacted at Westminster were exploited to the full.[7] During the second half of the 1850s the borough authorities began to exert a profoundly important impact on Plymouth's townscape and it is the purpose of this essay to examine the means by which the local urban environment was both shaped and managed by a local authority which developed a determinedly interventionist role.

Urban Management in Plymouth before 1854

In Plymouth, as elsewhere, the outmoded mechanisms by which environmental improvements could be effected in the eighteenth and early nineteenth century may have been adequate in pre-industrial times, but the onset of rapid population increase and rural-to-urban migration on a hitherto unprecedented scale, quickly exposed the deficiencies and shortcomings of the old system. This 'old system' usually centred on an Improvement Commission such as that established in Plymouth in 1770 by Act of Parliament. The powers of the Plymouth Commission were redefined and amended in a series of subsequent measures in 1772, 1774, 1815, and finally in 1824. Under the terms of this legislation, the Commissioners were empowered to levy a household rate and to use the revenue thereby secured to provide adequate lighting and paving of the town's streets. In addition, they could provide for the installation of drains and sewers, and arrange for street cleansing. Capital projects could be funded by raising loans against the security of the rates revenue. The Improvement Commission comprised the mayor, the borough recorder, the aldermen and common council, together with a further thirty-eight elected ratepayers.[8] But despite the wide franchise and apparently democratic character of this body, it possessed no power to control new development in Plymouth. It was only possible to intervene retro- spectively to correct the worst defects in the built environment.[9] Moreover, despite having powers of compulsory purchase in the older, overcrowded districts of Plymouth, the Improvement Commission repeatedly drew back from any attempt to deal effectively with acute environmental deficiencies. Many of those serving on the Commission were themselves owners of slum property—rented out to Plymouth's labouring classes. Such landlords were hardly likely to show enthusiasm for schemes of urban improvement which might entail self-imposed expenses.

Yet it was precisely during the period when this largely impotent and ineffective managerial body was in office that the population of Plymouth began to experience dramatic growth. At the first census in 1801, the population of the town stood at just above 16,000. By 1851 it totalled 52,000, and by the close of the Victorian era in 1901, it had reached 107,000. Thus in only a century the town's population had grown by 568 per cent. During the early years of the nineteenth century this massive increase in population was not matched by the building of extra dwellings. Exceptional levels of overcrowding resulted as large houses vacated by the middle classes in the old commercial core of the town slithered down the social ladder to become sub-divided and multi-occupied. The process was noted by Robert Rawlinson when he inspected Plymouth on behalf of the General Board of Health in 1852:

Many houses which were erected as residences for the nobility and gentry of the town are now the abode of the improvident, the vagrant, the vicious and the unfortunate.[10]

Building densities in the vicinity of Sutton Harbour were, of course, traditionally very high. Map evidence indicates an average of thirty-two houses to the acre.[11] (Figure 22). But while such dwellings were occupied by single family units, this kind of close-packed environment was tolerable. The census of 1851 indicates, however, the scale of deterioration which by then had occurred. In New Street, near the Barbican, some twenty-three houses accommodated 598 people—an average of twenty-six occupants per dwelling.[12] 'A dirty, blackguard, inconvenient place, and the approaches are mean and filthy in the extreme',[13] commented a local newspaper. Other blackspots included Basket Street, where there were on average twenty people per house, Stillman Street with fifteen, and Lower Street with thirteen. But even these extraordinarily high average figures can mask the true scale of the squalor. Thus, for example, in a single rear court off Stillman Street, there were 171 individuals enumerated in just six houses (none of which possessed any form of drainage and all sharing a single standpipe for their supply of water).[14]

Wealthier households had moved out to the more salubrious dwellings in the Princess Square area (where there were only eleven houses to the acre),[15] or even further afield to the suburbs on the northern edge of the town. Here they had escaped the worst ravages of the cholera epidemic of 1832 which claimed 779 lives in Plymouth—the overwhelming majority drawn from the crowded courts and alleys around Sutton Harbour.[16]

Edwin Chadwick's massive report on the *Sanitary Condition of the Labouring Population* published in 1842 began at last to focus national attention on the problem of urban environments.[17] Although initially the government's response to Chadwick's vast twelve-volume 'blue book' had been to operate the customary delaying tactic of appointing a Royal Commission which then produced two further reports (in 1843 and 1845) on the *State of Large Towns and Populous Districts*,[18] another, rather more significant, outcome was the propagation of intense local interest in England's urban environments. Branches of the Health of Towns Association sprang up everywhere and the more enterprising amongst them sponsored street-by-street surveys of conditions in their own boroughs.[19]

Thus in November, 1847, the Plymouth Health of Towns Association— largely through the tireless efforts of the Unitarian Minister the Reverend W.J. Odgers—produced its hard-hitting report on the sanitary condition of the borough. The *Odgers Report* (as it has come to be known) amounts to a major

The reform of urban management

Fig. 22 Building density in central Plymouth, 1855-60. From O.S. 1:2500. Sheet CXXIII.12. Surveyed 1855–60, printed 1886 (Courtesy of H.M. Ordnance Survey, Southampton)

indictment of the urban environment.[20] Of the town's 4,930 dwellings, some 2,200 were shown to possess neither a privy nor a water closet, and 1,763 were not served by any kind of drainage.

Dwellings were appallingly overcrowded and a total of 3,606 Plymouth households (together comprising 11,453 people) occupied single-room dwellings. The *Report* paid particular attention to the inadequacies of the existing Improvement Commission in failing to ensure that new development was properly constructed and serviced. Thus Union Street and the Octagon —built partly on reclaimed land as a link between Plymouth and the neighbouring town of Stonehouse—were shown to suffer from flooding. This was because parts of the street lay below sea level at higher tides, and some of the cellars of the houses on the southern side of the street were regularly inundated with sea water.[21] Inevitably infectious diseases such as scarlet fever, dysentry, whooping cough and tuberculosis were endemic in Plymouth.[22]

Local surveys of the kind carried out in Plymouth ultimately helped to persuade a reluctant Westminster government to introduce the first Public Health Act which was passed in 1848. But even this measure was overtaken by a second, and even more savage cholera epidemic which flared up first in Scotland and London, and eventually hit Plymouth in 1849. That year some 3,360 cases of the disease were registered in the town and, between July and October alone, some 819 people died.[23] As a port, Plymouth was especially vulnerable and the disease was almost certainly introduced via an emigrant ship embarked in London, but calling in the Sound to collect additional passengers.[24] The scale of the damage which cholera inflicted on the town may be blamed, however, upon the exceptionally poor quality of the local urban environment. The streets identified by Odgers two years earlier as particularly deleterious were precisely those where the cholera death-toll was heaviest. Yet though Plymouth sustained the seventh-highest cholera mortality rate in Britain, and despite the overwhelming evidence yielded by the *Odgers Report*, Plymouth's entrenched old Improvement Commission and the Town Council both resisted the adoption of the 1848 Public Health Act for six acrimonious and bitter years.

It took a petition from the local Ratepayer's Association plus an average deathrate in excess of twenty three per thousand over a seven-year period to prompt the General Board of Health in London to agree to a Public Health Inquiry in Plymouth, with a view to imposing the terms of the Public Health Act upon the Borough.[25] Robert Rawlinson conducted the hearings in the Guildhall in January 1852 and published his findings the following year.[26] The Improvement Commission and particularly its chairman, William Mortimer, reluctant to surrender the power and influence they had become accustomed to wielding, vigorously opposed all attempts to adopt the 1848 Act in Plymouth. When defeat finally came in 1854, and the old reactionary Commission was swept away to be replaced by a newly-elected, liberal-minded local Board of Health, Mortimer began a life-long campaign of opposition to the activities of the new regime. He directed a flood of complaints against the local board, and later the town council (after the two bodies merged). His letters survive amongst the extensive files of correspondence relating to public health and local government in Plymouth preserved in the Public Record Office. By the 1870s, Whitehall civil servants appear to have grown accustomed to Mr. Mortimer's lengthy letters of complaint—often extending to 24 pages of characteristic pale-blue foolscap. Ultimately Mortimer's entreaties were accorded no more than a cursory response and were frequently minuted 'scarcely warrants an answer', or 'another of Mr. M.'s tirades'.[27] But in addition to the sustained and nagging opposition of disaffected citizens like Mortimer, in Plymouth, the local authorities were also obliged to take into account the views and needs of the Admiralty, the Royal Marines, the Board of Ordnance and, in due course, the Great Western Dock Company.

Land within the borough owned by these various interests was often the subject of considerable dispute when plans such as those for the supply of piped water and the installation of sewers were being formulated. Urban reform in Plymouth was certainly neither easy nor straightforward. But the days when power was wielded so effectively by a group wedded to the principle of inaction were long gone and, from 1854, nothing could seriously halt progress towards an ever more comprehensive system of environmental management by municipal authority in Plymouth.

Urban Management by Plymouth's Local Board of Health

From the moment of its formation, Plymouth's newly elected Board of Health was in the vanguard of new thinking on the kinds of powers thought necessary in order to effect improvements in the built environment. The Board quickly made use of the relatively limited powers available under the terms of the national legislation to frame bye-laws tailored to meet specific local needs. Controls first sought by the Plymouth Board often became universal later as they were built into new Acts of Parliament in wider legislative developments. In a very real sense, therefore, Plymouth's mid-Victorian experience helped to shape the more overtly interventionist national environmental policies which reached the statute book towards the end of the century.

In the 1850s the scale of Plymouth's problems—worsened by years of neglect under the old Improvement Commission—may have been enough to convince the Board of Health that direct management was now unavoidable.

A 'special works committee' was established to explore the means by which the sewers and the streets of the borough could be improved.[28]

Re-negotiating the terms of Mr. F.W.Harris's contract to supply the borough with brooms for 'cleansing the streets' at the rate of seventeen shillings a dozen was one thing,[29] but the installation of properly metalled road surfaces was quite another. Members of the committee quickly recognised that the task would take years to complete. On 11 July 1855, the committee's chairman, Thomas Gill, called for a survey of Plymouth streets in order to establish an order of priorities.[30] An array of difficulties were encountered which seriously impeded progress. One of the most intractable arose because of the lack of a clear definition of the term 'highway'. In cases where a street was a 'highway', the cost of paving technically fell on borough resources. Elsewhere, it was the responsibility of the owners of property located in the street. But in Plymouth there were numerous roadways which had:

> ... in many instances been open to the public and used as thoroughfares for years, and yet they are in a very imperfect state, with no metalling or even ballast on them, and they are scarcely passable for any vehicle. By some it is contended that such streets or roadways are *Highways* inasmuch as they have been long open to and used by the public, whilst others contend that they are not highways because they have never been put in order.[31]

Even when such legal complexities had been resolved, the process of improvement was slow. In years past, the Improvement Commission had paved roadways cheaply using the relatively inferior stone quarried at Staddon Down (of which the borough was leaseholder). Recognising that the Staddon stone surfaces had already deteriorated, the Board of Health was faced with the task not only of paving previously unpaved and newly formed streets, but also of replacing some existing paving with the more durable Dartmoor granite and Hoe limestone. Between 1857-66 a sum in excess of £45,000 was borrowed on the security of the rates in order to install granite paving in a number of Plymouth's key thoroughfares.[32] (Fig. 23). Meanwhile other, less demanding projects were also undertaken in the town. Thus, in 1856, a special committee had been formed to improve the labels and house numbering in the town. Some 340 new street labels were set up and 2,300 dwellings were re-numbered in a scheme which took several years to complete.[33]

At the same time a completely new sewerage system was devised by the borough's newly appointed surveyor-engineer, Robert Hodge, and his proposals were submitted to Whitehall on 24th July, 1855. Difficulties were

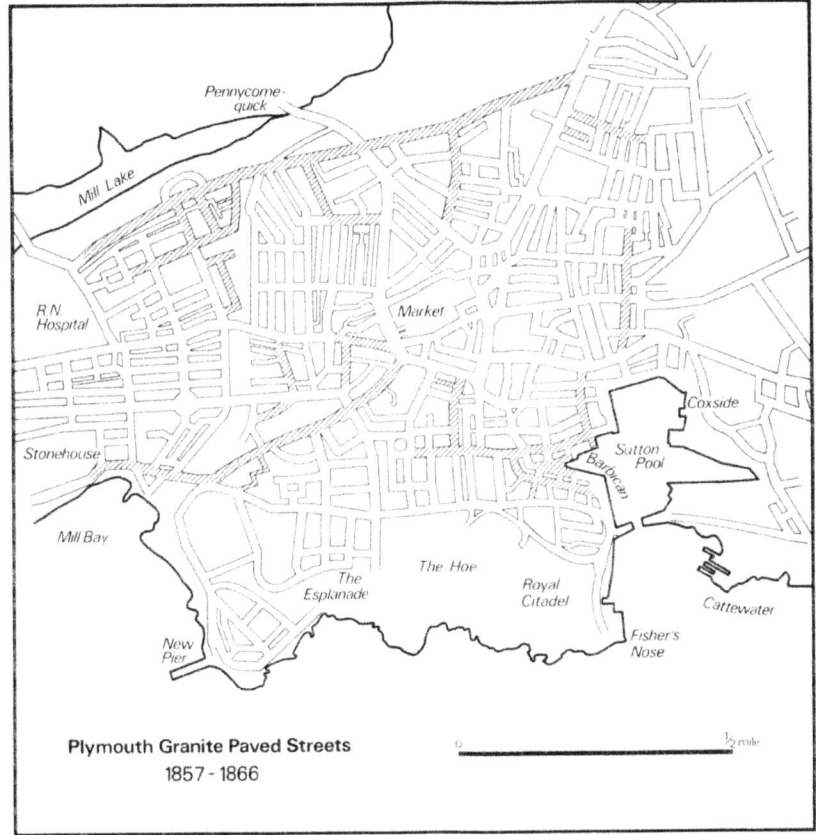

Fig. 23 *Plymouth granite paved streets, 1857–1866*

encountered in obtaining a tracing of the Ordnance Survey ten-feet-to-the-mile plan of Plymouth, and as an interim arrangement, it was agreed that the scheme could be shown on the five-feet-to-the-mile drawing which the Board of Health in Plymouth possessed.[34] In the event this scale proved inadequate for showing the diameter of mains pipes and the gradient of slopes upon which the system relied.[35] Even after the Board of Ordnance provided the large-scale drawings, further serious delays were encountered because the proposed new outfalls beyond Sutton Harbour in the eastern section, and beyond Millbay in the western section, required the sanction of the Admiralty.

Although broadly supportive, the latter nonetheless raised a string of minor objections and caveats.[36] In addition the Commandant of the Royal Marine Barracks submitted objections,[37] and he was quickly followed by the Board of Ordnance.[38] And the Board of Management of the Great Western Dock Company presented Hodge with yet more difficulties.[39] Solutions were not easily found and progress in installing the main axial pipework of the new sewerage system was not complete until the 1860s. By this time, however, several principal streets were already linked into the new network (Fig. 24) and thereafter most of Plymouth's streets were gradually afforded the benefits of mains drainage and sewerage.

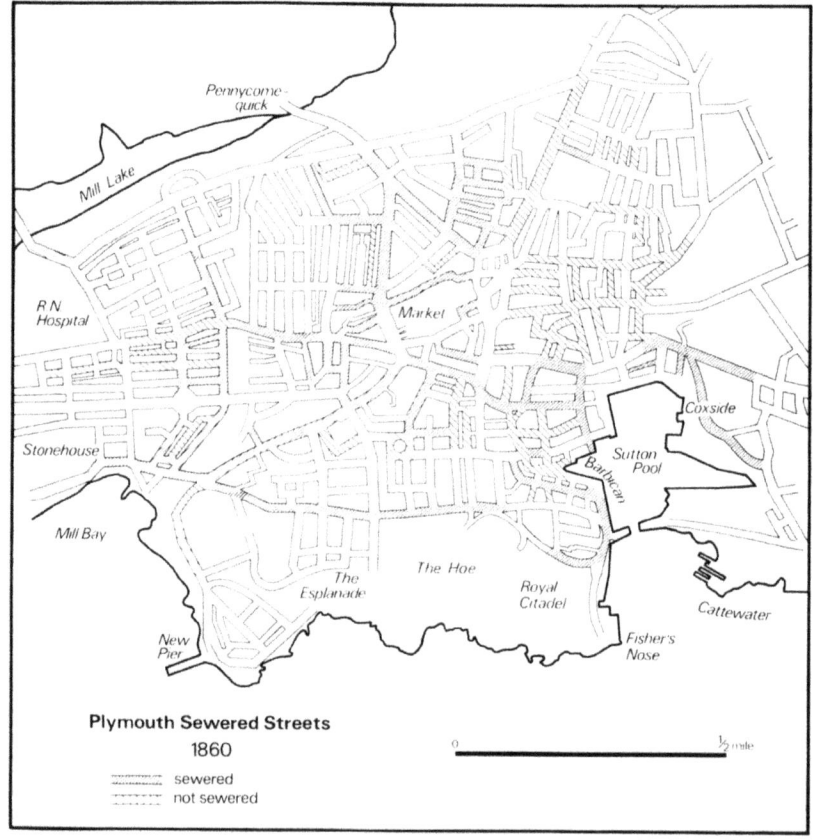

Fig. 24 *Plymouth sewered streets, 1860*

Under the 72nd section of the 1848 Public Health Act Plymouth's Board of Health quickly framed bye-laws defining minimum widths for newly formed streets. Major thoroughfares were to be no less than thirty feet in width, while rear lanes were to be no less than fourteen feet.[40] As early as June, 1855, a proposal to develop an area of Coxside was rejected by the local Board on the grounds that the proposed streets were only twelve and a half feet in width.[41] Indeed, the terms of the local legislation appear to have been rigidly applied and development plans which failed to comply by as little as half an inch could expect to be rejected.

Measures to control the siting of slaughterhouses and the keeping of livestock were also obtained. Plymouth's role as a regional market centre, and as a supply depot for the victualling of ships, inevitably meant that an unusually large volume of both livestock and deadstock was handled in the town. The environmental consequences in terms of filth in the streets and the noxious odours from abattoirs were now, at last, to be tackled. Private slaughterhouses were to be licensed by the local authority and, in later years, when premises changed hands, licenses were sometimes revoked as part of the Board's policy to confine such premises to certain well-defined parts of the town.[42] It was, however, harder to prevent the erection of new abattoirs in unsuitable locations and, as a letter from Charles Whiteford, Plymouth's Town Clerk, makes clear, applications to build new premises were frequently received:

> There are at present nineteen private slaughterhouses in different parts of the town licensed by the local Board of Health, and several applications have been made for permission to build further establishments.[43]

In 1861, in order to obviate the need for further private slaughterhouses, the Board sought permission to erect a municipal abattoir and cowshed inside an enclosure on the north side of Glanville Street, directly opposite the entrance to the Tavistock Road cattle market. Local protests, in the form of a petition presented to the Home Secretary by residents of the Glanville Street neighbourhood, argued that such a building would be unacceptable.[44] But the local Board pointed out that it was, in fact, the most logical site:

> The Tavistock Road is the great northern entrance to the town along which large numbers of cattle are daily driven from the country to the cattle market, or to be slaughtered in the town.[45]

Eventually the Local Government Act Office in Whitehall was persuaded to allow Plymouth to raise a loan of £1,250 and the municipal slaughterhouse was duly erected. The demand for more privately built premises was thereby reduced and, in an ingeniously indirect manner, the local authority had managed to impose a control on the siting of a new facility. Indeed, controls exercised both directly (by the licence system), and indirectly (by building municipally owned facilities), on the siting of slaughterhouses represent an early form of land-use zoning which was later extended to other urban activities, such as the manufacture of bonemeal and fertiliser, and the chemical works. The effluvia and atmospheric pollution emitted from such establishments gave rise to many complaints during the 1850s and 1860s.[46] Gradually Plymouth's Inspector of Nuisances reduced the problem by vigorously employing his right to serve the owners of offending establishments with 'nuisance abatement' orders.[47] Proceedings against those who failed to

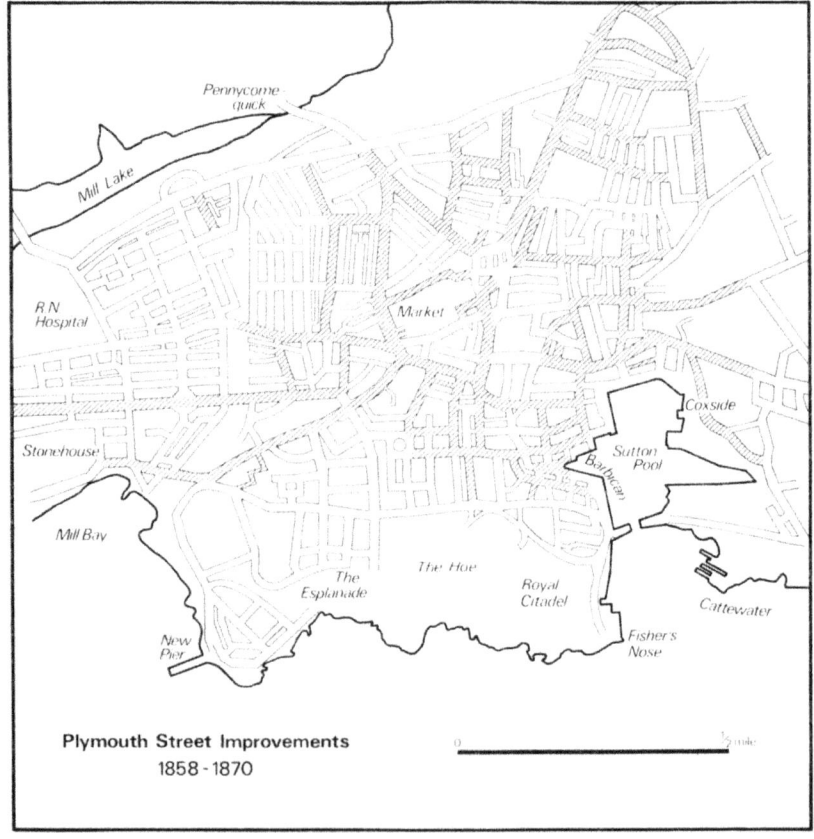

Fig. 25 *Plymouth street improvements, 1858–1870*

respond were invariably taken and, by this means, noxious trades were gradually persuaded to locate in areas where their impact upon residential and commercial property was minimised.

Beginning in March 1856, the Board of Health embarked on an ambitious programme of street improvements to ease the flow of traffic through thoroughfares impeded by haphazard building encroachment and irregular alignments.[48] A lack of control exercised by the *Improvement Commission* since 1770 had rendered some key streets virtually impassable by modern wheeled vehicles and the Board's immediate task was to acquire by purchase all the buildings and parcels of land which had previously been allowed to intrude onto the carriageway. Thereafter, a programme of demolition, followed by the realignment of the road and the installation of new paving, was put into operation. There can be little doubt of the dramatic impact of this kind of improvement in the mid-Victorian town. Although still considered (by the Medical Officer of Health) to be one of the most congested boroughs in southern England in the 1930s, the problem in Plymouth would have been still more intractable had there been no street improvement scheme in the 1850s and 1860s. In all, the local Board of Health was occupied with the implementation of its improvement programme for well over a decade, such were the complexities of purchasing offending properties and effecting the improvements in the tangle of medieval streets near the core of the town (Fig. 25).

Building Controls and Street Alignments

Within months of its establishment, Plymouth's Board of Health recognised the need for powers both to control the standard of new buildings erected in the borough, and to purchase compulsorily (in cases where the owner refused to sell voluntarily) those properties impeding a carriageway.

They found they possessed neither. Although under the terms of the Public Health Act of 1848, developers were obliged to submit for approval all plans of proposed new buildings, it was in theory only possible for the local Board to insist on changes in the proposals for drains; there were no powers to control street alignments, building heights or the standards of construction. As early as 1855, however, the Plymouth Board attempted to exercise a degree of control beyond that legally allowed by the 1848 Act. Thus, in a number of cases, plans submitted by developers were returned because the Board objected to the heights of new buildings being proposed. Written protests sent by Plymouth builders survive amongst the General Board of Health correspondence in the Public Record Office.[49] When the controversy was at its height, the secretary of the Plymouth

Board, William Eastlake, sought clarification on the matter:

> A question has arisen with the local Board here as to whether they have any powers to regulate the height of houses either being rebuilt, or newly built. This question is one of much importance in this borough where there are many narrow streets in which it frequently happens that old houses are rebuilt and the local board are desirous to know if they have the power to regulate the height of building in proportion to the width of the street.[50]

In reply the General Board noted that:

> Local boards have in several instances endeavoured to regulate the directions of streets, but as they have no power in the matter beyond that which is given them by the Public Health Act, they have been informed by this Board that they had no power to interfere to that extent. The same answer applies to the height of houses and to all other matters of this kind which are not expressly mentioned in the Act.[51]

It may be noted that this ruling on behalf of the General Board was arrived at only after a degree of agonising as Eastlake's letter ascended the Whitehall chain of command. Marginal notes, written by various officials, clearly indicate that there was considerable sympathy with Plymouth's desire to control the heights of buildings and, in March 1855, when revisions to the Public Health Act and a new Nuisances Removal Bill were being drafted, William Eastlake again wrote on behalf of the Plymouth Board to urge the inclusion of clauses to extend very considerably the range of powers which local boards might exercise.[52] Indeed, less than a month later, the Plymouth Board requested a meeting with representatives of the General Board to discuss the extension of the powers embodied in the new bills. An exchange of ideas and counter-ideas continued for almost eighteen months.[53] But the Public Health Amendment Bill was finally shelved in 1857 and the powers of local boards were not significantly extended until the passing of the new *Local Government Act* in 1858.

Meanwhile there were clashes between the local Board and Plymouth developers over the matter of street alignments. For example, in February 1855, F.W. Pym had submitted plans to develop a seven-acre 'green-field' site on the edge of the town. His proposals were returned together with a range of suggested alterations to the width and level of the proposed streets, as well as the position and size of the drains. In addition, the Board had altered the alignment of the two axial streets in Pym's development. Messrs. Whiteford, Bennett and Tucker (Pym's solicitors) took up the matter with the General Board of Health arguing that the local Board did not possess the legal authority to insist on the changes. Ultimately Pym won his case, but again the notes written in the margins of the correspondence indicate an appreciation of the local Board's position by the civil servants in Whitehall. Their official reply was clearly very carefully worded:

> The Government Board cannot undertake to give an opinion as to the legality of the proceedings of a local board of health when the opinion is asked for on the part of a private individual. The proper course for your client to pursue is to instruct counsel to determine whether it should appear that the local board are exceeding their power in requiring that the direction of the streets in question should be altered.[54]

Few Plymouth builders would have wanted to risk the delays and expense of litigation and the local Board therefore wielded considerable *de facto* control over the alignment of streets formed after February, 1855. The town's regular grid of straight mid-Victorian streets, monotonously identical in width, owes a great deal to the interventionist stance of the local Board of Health and should not necessarily be interpreted as a builders' device to make maximum use of the space available. Indeed, several local builders complained that the Board's preoccupation with standard straight streets' incurred a loss of land and thereby a loss of money to the developer.[55] But straight streets were more easily cleansed and serviced and the rigid geometry of Plymouth's Victorian townscape is a clear and lasting reflection of positive urban management exercised well in advance of the establishment of national legal controls.

Powers of Compulsory Purchase

In June 1856, the Plymouth Board of Health complained to the President of the General Board, Sir Benjamin Hall, that in adopting the terms of the Public Health Act of 1848, the powers of the old Improvement Commission to 'acquire property other than by agreement' (that is, by compulsory purchase) had inadvertantly been repealed.[56] A desire was expressed that these extinguished powers might be restored under the terms of the Public Health Amendment Bill which was then under consideration. As noted earlier, this legislation did not proceed, and by 1858 the problem in Plymouth had become acute. Progress in the programme of street improvements was seriously interrupted by occupiers and owners who steadfastly refused to agree to sell their slum property. In January, 1858, William Eastlake again alerted Sir Benjamin to the problem:

> The local Board of Health find themselves repeatedly in difficulty owing to their being unable to avail themselves of the power to purchase premises (under certain circumstances) compulsorily, given them by 5 Geo: 4 cap 22 [the old Improvement Act] ... I am now requested to submit that, as it was entirely

through the inadventure of the General Board that the local Board was thus deprived of very important powers, the General Board should take such measures as may be necessary to restore these powers to the local Board.[57]

Although no action was taken specifically on behalf of Plymouth, the new Local Government Act, which reached the statute book later that year, at last included clauses allowing compulsory purchase under strictly controlled circumstances. Two years of pressure from the Plymouth Board of Health may well have played a part in securing this modest extension of local authority power. The new Act in fact established a system whereby a Standing Order of the House of Commons enabled local boards of health to identify (in a single annual list published during December) all properties which were to be purchased compulsorily during the following year. In March 1860, William Eastlake sought clarification from the secretariat at the new Local Government Act Office, which had assumed the responsibilities of the now-dissolved General Board of Health. Eastlake pointed out that if a slum property was privately demolished in the early part of the year, the local board had no power to acquire it (other than by agreement) until November or December. By this time 'probably the premises would be rebuilt and all chance of purchasing, except at greatly increased cost, would be lost'.[58] The Plymouth Board requested permission to publish lists more frequently of properties earmarked for compulsory purchase. Although this was refused, and despite the obvious inconvenience of confining to December all notices of intent to purchase property compulsorily, Plymouth prepared for its first compulsory purchase orders. Under the terms of clause 75 of the 1858 Local Government Act, the intentions of the Plymouth Board of Health were advertised locally once a week, for three consecutive weeks in November 1860. Plans were made available for public perusal. Thereafter the owners of the properties in question were personally served with notices of compulsory purchase and the Local Government Act Office was informed of these actions in January 1861. But William Eastlake was called to London to consult with officials in the Local Government Act Office and he was required to furnish proof that proper notice had been served. He was advised that a Public Inquiry by a Local Government Inspector would be held in Plymouth. Thus in May, 1861, Henry Austin presided at the Inquiry in Plymouth's Guildhall. He afterwards submitted his recommendation to the Home Secretary, Sir George Cornewell-Lewis, and a Provisional Order was drawn up to be submitted for Parliamentary approval. When this was obtained on 15 July 1861, the local Board was at last permitted to take possession of the thirty-four properties identified some nine months earlier.[59] The process could hardly have been more protracted and cumbersome. Only the most determinedly interventionist local authority might be expected to undertake such proceedings. In Plymouth, however, despite the limitations and difficulties of the system, the need for improvement was such that the Board saw no alternative. Further Compulsory Purchase inquiries followed almost annually until 1870. Each time, a Local Government Inspector visited Plymouth, and presided over a local inquiry. When written objections were raised, the Inspector visited every property in person, prior to the meeting in the Guildhall.[60] Since most of the dwellings were not actually occupied by their owners, but were instead rented to tenants who enjoyed virtually no security of tenure, the objections raised by householders were rarely heeded once the acquiescence of the property *owner* had been secured. On 13th March 1865, Robert Morgan informed the Home Secretary, Sir George Grey, of his conclusions after conducting the latest Inquiry in Plymouth:

> I have visited each locality proposed to be interfered with. Owing to the increased amount of traffic and the narrowness of the streets referred to, these alterations are much required, and will, when completed, form most important local improvements.[61]

Scarcely any mention is made of the families displaced through the compulsory purchase of their dwellings, and certainly there were no means by which assistance in securing alternative accommodation might be afforded. And yet it is clear that, in the 1860s and 1870s, the compulsory purchase of property in Plymouth displaced several hundred residents (Fig. 26). In the short and medium term there can be no doubt that this process may actually have exacerbated the problem of overcrowding as the dispossessed families sought accommodation in adjacent courts and alleys. After all, few could afford to live too far from their place of employment. So, even new housing, built on the old Barley Estate on the north-west of the town in the 1860s, was multi-occupied within months of its completion. It may well be that this is a reflection of the additional pressure on available accommodation induced by the activities of the local authority. Until the advent of municipal housing in 1896, scarcely any thought appears to have been given to the social impact of interventionist urban management policies in Plymouth. But notwithstanding the gruesome social deficiencies of the compulsory purchase programme, the environmental improvements carried through by Plymouth's municipal authorities after 1854 certainly exerted a dramatic and lasting impact on the townscape. They also ultimately influenced the health of the population. By the 1880s, the local level of mortality had reduced to only 14.6 per thousand—lower than any other urban area of comparable size, and substantially below that of Manchester (21 per thousand) or Newcastle (23 per thousand).[62]

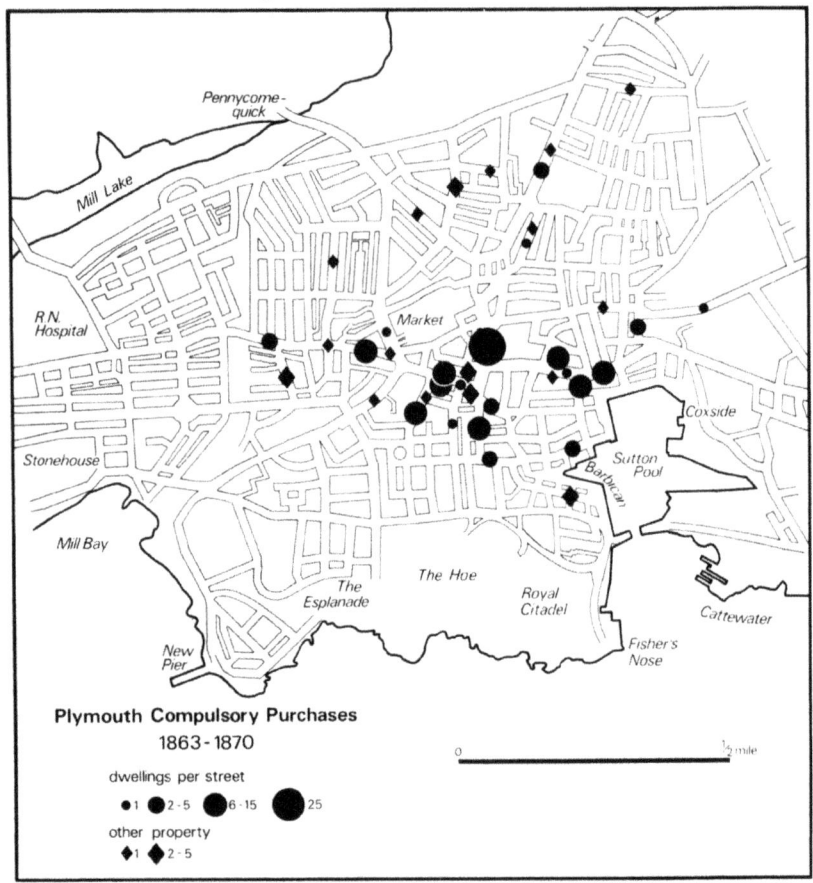

Fig. 26 *Plymouth compulsory purchases, 1863–1870*

Capital Projects and the Raising of Finance

By the late 1850s municipal control in Plymouth encompassed not only highways, sewers, drains and new development proposals, but also the maintenance of pleasure grounds, public conveniences, and public baths and wash-houses. New pleasure grounds were created including the park on Plymouth Hoe on land once belonging to the Royal Ordnance. The wages of a special Hoe-policeman were included in the maintenance budget for the park.[63]

The reform of urban management

As in other towns, the scope of municipal activity was in part determined by the increases in revenue derived from the collection of borough rates.

Additional dwellings—especially those erected for the wealthier members of the community—helped to swell Plymouth's annual rate income to £166,429 by 1871.[64] Nevertheless, such funds were insufficient to finance the larger environmental schemes being contemplated by the Board of Health and the Town Council in the mid-Victorian period. Perhaps the most significant was the extension of the supply of piped water to Plymouth households which was undertaken in the 1860s. Hitherto the town had depended on the supplies available from the sixteenth-century leats which tapped the river Meavy on Dartmoor, together with supplies drawn from a number of wells located in the area of Sutton Harbour. Demand had outstripped the capacity of the leat, while supplies drawn from wells were subject to contamination. Although a small storage reservoir was built at Honicknowle (the Crownhill reservoir) in 1852, supplies were still limited and unpredictable. Thus, in September 1858, Thomas Skardon, the Mayor of Plymouth, applied to the Local Government Act Office for permission to borrow £7,670.9s.0d. on the security of the rates revenue in order to build a new, seven-million gallon reservoir at Hartley.[65] This was the first of a long series of loans secured in this manner (Fig. 27). Indeed, by the early 1870s, the borough had sought borrowing facilities totalling more than £110,500.[66] Permission was customarily granted only after an inquiry had been undertaken by the sanitary engineers on the staff of the Local Government Act Office. Initially, building work on the new Hartley reservoir was delayed by the strike of local masons in 1859 and 1860, but the project was eventually completed in 1861 (Fig. 28). Additional funds were thereafter employed to extend the network of supply to the majority of Plymouth households. By 1870 the local authorities had expended more than £42,000 on the borough water supply and when additional borrowing was required, Whitehall decided to dispense with the need for further central government authorisation. The municipally owned waterworks yielded a net annual income to the borough of £7,700 by 1872 and this was already employed as security for raising further funds to extend and improve the network. When the new fortifications at Crownhill were erected in 1869, the leat serving the municipal reservoir was diverted and the flow was actually thereby improved. Indeed, supplies remained adequate until the mid-1880s when a loan of £31,500 was secured to commence work on another new reservoir at Roborough.[67]

Funds for capital projects were raised by mortgaging not only revenue, but also the capital assets of the town. Thus, in 1865, Corporation property was put up as security to fund the improvement of the butchers' stalls in the

BOROUGH OF PLYMOUTH.

To EXCAVATORS
AND
BUILDERS.

The TOWN COUNCIL of PLYMOUTH are desirous to receive

TENDERS
FOR CONSTRUCTING A
RESERVOIR,
EXCAVATING GROUND,
AND
BUILDING BOUNDARY WALLS,
AND OTHER WORKS,
AT HARTLEY, NEAR PLYMOUTH.

The Drawings and Specification may be seen at the Town Surveyor's Office, No. 5, Buckwell Street, between the hours of 10 a.m. and 2 p.m. until THURSDAY, the 22nd day of SEPTEMBER, 1859.

Tenders to be delivered at the Town Surveyor's Office, on or before 11 a.m. on Friday, 23rd September inst.

The Council will not engage to accept the lowest or any of the Tenders, and the party whose Tender may be accepted will be required to enter into an agreement, and give security for the execution of his Contract.

ROBERT HODGE, C.E.,

Dated 9th September, 1859.   SURVEYOR TO THE PLYMOUTH CORPORATION.

Fig. 27   Part of a Government Sanitary Engineer's Report on Plymouth's need for a new reservoir, 1858 (P.R.O., HLG2/61/15230)

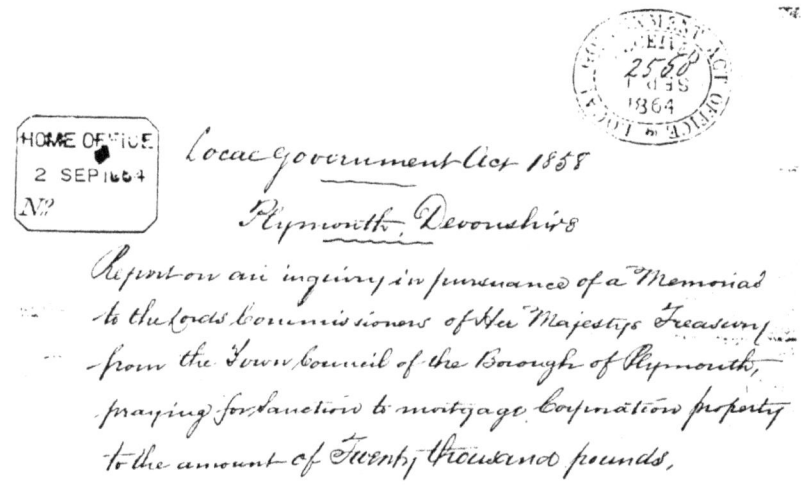

Fig. 28 *Advertisement for tenders to build Hartley Reservoir, Plymouth, 1859*

borough market and the rebuilding of the town flour mills.[68] In 1870, Plymouth's Town Clerk applied to the Treasury for permission to mortgage both the borough rates, and some corporate freehold property, in order to raise £30,000 to build a new Guildhall and municipal offices:

The necessity of erecting a new Guildhall with suitable Law Courts and a proper Council Room and offices for the administration of Justice and the transaction of public business had been recognised for upwards of thirty years, but owing to the large expenditure which has been necessarily incurred by the Council and the Local Board in different public works and sanitary improvements, the Council has not been in a position sooner to enter upon so large an expenditure.[69]

At this point the elderly ex-chairman of the Improvement Commission, William Mortimer—out of office for the past sixteen years—fired off his final salvo of criticism. In a characteristically lengthy letter, written in a noticeably less-accomplished hand than hitherto, Mortimer relentlessly castigated the local authority for allegedly mis-using both its legal powers and borough resources. Sinister ulterior motives were alluded to, and the Lords of the Treasury were urged to withold their consent to Plymouth's proposal to mortgage the rates again.[70] But it was all to no avail. The new civic complex was built to a self-confident italianate design obtained by public competition, thereby setting the seal on the municipalisation of Plymouth's mid-Victorian townscape.

In later Victorian times, the local authority assumed an ever broadening social role. By 1887, borrowing facilities were being sought to purchase a site adjacent to the Tavistock road for a Science, Art & Technical college, which was then erected using funds secured through public subscription as well as loans raised on the security of corporation assets.[71] In the 1890s all the old urban burial grounds were closed and the corporation purchased a large site at Eggbuckland for use as a new borough cemetery.[72] And finally, in 1898, Plymouth Corporation began to issue stock in order to raise further capital to finance its ever increasing programme of public works. By 1900 more than £108,000 worth of stock had already been issued.[73]

Conclusion

Although it cannot be claimed that Plymouth's Victorian townscape was the product of planning in the modern sense, neither was it the result of laissez-faire. Certain elements in the configuration and pattern of the built environment disclose the firm hand of environmental management and control, exercised with an increasing sureness of touch by a determinedly interventionist local authority from 1854 onwards. Such a conclusion may appear to contradict the orthodox view that the 1848 Public Health Act was a largely ineffective piece of legislation which was resisted by fiercely independent local councils. But this is a view of English history seen primarily from a national standpoint—from Westminster looking outwards—which sees the anti-centralisation sentiments of Victorian society in terms of their effects upon central institutions. Thus we refer to the dilution of the powers of the General Board of Health or the Local Government Act Office caused by an anti-centralist feeling. But this obscures the fact that the same popular attitude could also be the origin of a very considerable degree of positive municipal action. Radical local authorities were often anxious to demonstrate that they had no real need of central direction. Once enabling legislation had been enacted, some provincial towns readily exploited their new powers and strongly argued the case for further national provisions. In the absence of these, local authorities sought to develop their own bye-laws and to pilot their own local acts through Parliament. Local pride, local knowledge, local incentive and unique local circumstances all appeared to demand local solutions. Moreover, the benefits of municipal activity were generally measured on a practical, rather than on a theoretical plane and it was therefore possible to be committed ideologically to the virtues of 'self-help' and laissez-faire, while at the same time accepting the ever broadening role of the local authority in managing the urban environment and controlling its use.

As recently as 1982 it was argued that the failure of the 1848 Public Health Act was merely the most notorious of numerous episodes, both national and local, in which the administrative dynamic dashed itself to pieces against implacable public opinion.[74] From a national point of view, such a conclusion may be acceptable, but in failing to take into account the extent to which the powers enshrined in the 1848 Act were actually exploited in practice in particular boroughs, it provides only a very partial view of reality. The need for studies of practical administrative developments in individual towns could hardly have been more forcibly demonstrated. In Plymouth, far from the administrative dynamic being 'dashed to pieces', the need for additional powers was repeatedly recognised and the Act, together with its successors, was skilfully used in reshaping and improving the mid-Victorian urban environment.

Notes

1. See for example: E. Gauldie, *Cruel Habitations: A History of Working Class Housing, 1780-1918* (1974); S.M.Gaskell, *Building control: National Legislation and the Introduction of Local Bye-laws in Victorian Britain* (1983); A. Sutcliffe, 'The growth of public intervention in the British urban environment during the nineteenth century' in J.H. Johnson & C.G. Pooley (eds.) *The Structure of Nineteenth-Century Cities* (1982),107-24.
2. D. Fraser, *Power and Authority in the Victorian City* (1979).
3. Fraser 1979 (see note 2). Also see A. Sutcliffe, *Towards the Planned City* (1981), 47-87.
4. P. Thane, 'Introduction' in P. Thane (ed.) *The Origins of British Social Policy* (1978), 11-20. Also see W. Ashworth, *The Genesis of Modern British Town Planning: A Study in Economic and Social History of the Nineteenth and Twentieth Centuries* (1954).
5. See N. McCord, 'Ratepayers and social policy' in P.Thane 1978 (see note 4), 21-35.
6. E.P. Hennock, 'Finance and politics in urban local government, 1835-1900' *Hist. J.* 6 (1963), 212-25; also see D. Fraser, 'Politics and the Victorian City', *Urban History Yearbook* (1979), 32-45.
7. See C.E. Welch, 'Municipal reform in Plymouth', *Trans. Devon. Ass.*, 96 (1964), 313-38; also see M. Brayshay & V. Pointon, 'Local politics and public health in mid-nineteenth century Plymouth', *Medical History*, 27 (1983), 162-78; and C. Gill, *Plymouth: A New History* Vol. II (1979), 107-16.
8. Welch 1964 (see note 7), 323-4. The ratepayers' representatives were eligible by virtue of a property qualification.

9. Brayshay & Pointon 1983 (see note 7), 166-7.
10. P.R.O., MH 13, 144/1082/53 Robert Rawlinson's draft report on Plymouth, 7 April 1853.
11. I am grateful to Mr. Brian Rogers for making these measurements using the O.S. 1:2500 plans of Plymouth (surveyed in 1890).
12. P.R.O., HO 107/1877 Census Enumerators Books, Plymouth 1851.
13. P[lymouth] and D[evonport] W[eekly] J[ournal], 17 May 1849, 3.
14. W.J. Odgers, A report on the sanitary condition of Plymouth (1847), 14.
15. See note 11.
16. See P.D.W.J., 15 Jan.1852, 8; and 22 Jan. 1852, 2-3.
17. See F.B. Smith, The People's Health, 1838-1918 (1979), 190-200; also Fraser 1979 (see note 2), 26-30.
18. C. Fraser Brockington, A Short History of Public Health (1956).
19. A. Briggs, The Age of Improvement (1959), 334-5, 441. Also see Gauldie 1974 (see note 1).
20. Odgers 1847 (see note 14).
21. P.R.O., MH 13, 145/2702/67 The government chief sanitary engineer finally visited Plymouth to advise on this problem in August 1867.
22. Brayshay & Pointon 1983 (see note 7), 170, and Table III.
23. P.D.W.J., 16 Aug–4 Oct 1849, also 13 Dec 1849.
24. P.D.W.J., 5 June 1849. The ship was the American Eagle bound for New York.
25. P.R.O., MH 13, 144/5249/52 Memorial from the ratepayers of Plymouth to the G[eneral] B[oard] of H[ealth], December, 1849. Also P.R.O., MH 13, 144/960/53 Thomas Stevens to the GBH 25 March 1853.
26. P.D.W.J., 22 Jan 1852. The Inquiry ran from 15-20 January 1852.
27. See for example: P.R.O., MH 13, 144/897/53; MH 13, 145/650/56; HLG, 2/61/20968; HLG, 2/62/102. The franchise was actually wider than that for Parliamentary representation.
28. P.R.O., MH 13, 144/3847 William Eastlake to the GBH 29 August 1854.
29. W.D.R.O., P4/A1 Borough of Plymouth, Minutes of the Proceedings of the Local Board of Health, 23 Jan. 1856.
30. P.R.O., MH 13, 144/2983 Report of the meeting of Plymouth's special works committee held II July 1855.
31. P.R.O., MH 13, 144/51 William Eastlake to the GBH, 5 Jan 1855.
32. P.R.O., MH 13, 145/1800 Charles Whiteford to Sir George Grey, 25 June 1864.
33. W.D.R.O., P4/A1-A3, Minutes, 2 July 1856.
34. P.R.O., MH 13, 144/5357 William Eastlake to the GBH, 23 Oct. 1854; also 5357 GBH to William Eastlake, 25 Oct. 1854; and 3073 Robert Hodge to the GBH, 24 July 1855.
35. P.R.O., MH 13, 144/3339 Robert Hodge to the GBH, 25 Aug. 1855; and 3340 GBH to Robert Hodge, 26 July 1856.
36. P.R.O., MH 13, 145/221 Lords Commissioners of the Admiralty to the GBH, 18 Jan. 1856.
37. P.R.O., MH 13, 145/4038 J.H. Gascoigne, Colonel Commandant of Royal Marine Barracks to the L[ocal] G[overnment] A[ct] O[ffice], 6 Oct. 1865.
38. P.R.O., MH 13, 145/4071 Colonel Connolly to LGAO, 16 Oct. 1865.

The reform of urban management 129

39. P.R.O., MH 13, 145/6198 Great Western Dock Company Memorial to the GBH, 8 July 1856; see also 2506 Robert Hodge to LGAO, 26 Nov. 1860, and 2481 Thomas Stevens to LGAO, 28 Oct. 1860.
40. W.D.R.O., P4/A1-A3, Minutes, 4 June 1855.
41. W.D.R.O., P4/A1-A3, Minutes, 2 Aug 1855.
42. P.R.O., MH 13, 145/2533 William Eastlake to LGAO, 16 Dec 1859.
43. P.R.O., MH 13, 145/428 Charles Whiteford to LGAO, 28 Feb. 1861.
44. P.R.O., MH 13, 145/267 Rev. H.A. Greaves to the Home Secretary, 14 Feb. 1861.
45. See note 43.
46. P.R.O., MH 13, 144/6019 H. Waddington to the President of GBH, 2 Dec 1854; also 340 E. James to Lord Palmerston, 25 Jan 1855. See also: *Western Morning News*, 18 March 1864, 'A Coxside Manufactury Indicted as a Nuisance'.
47. P.R.O., MH 13, 145/14797 William Symons to the GBH, 10 Dec. 1856. 'Duties of a Sanitary Inspector'.
48. P.R.O., MH 13, 145/981 William Eastlake to the GBH, 27 March 1856.
49. P.R.O., MH 13, 144/719 William Eastlake to the GBH, 22 Feb, 1855; see also W.D.R.O., P4/Al, Minutes, 4 June 1855.
50. P.R.O., MH 13, 144/804 William Eastlake to the GBH, 27 Feb 1855.
51. P.R.O., MH 13, 144/805 GBH to William Eastlake, 28 Feb 1855.
52. P.R.O., MH 13, 144/1102 William Eastlake to the GBH, 16 March 1855; 1496, 13 April 1855; and 1497, 14 April 1855.
53. P.R.O., MH 13, 144/3657 William Eastlake to the GBH, 28 Sept. 1855; 1818 William Eastlake to the GBH, 26 June 1856.
54. P.R.O., MH 13, 144/719 GBH to Messrs. Whiteford, Bennett & Tucker, 22 Feb. 1855.
55. P.R.O., MH 13, 145/1818 John Ambrose to the GBH, 2 June 1856.
56. P.R.O., MH 13, 144/3657 William Eastlake to the GBH, 28 Sept. 1855.
57. P.R.O., MH 13, 145/74 William Eastlake to the GBH, 11 Jan 1858.
58. P.R.O., MH 13, 145/518 William Eastlake to the LGAO, 1 March 1860.
59. P.R.O., MH 13, 145/5310 William Eastlake to the LGAO, 10 Jan 1861; also 1053, 30 May 1861. The Order was finally sent for signature on 15 July 1861.
60. See for example P.R.O., MH 13, 145/327 Charles Whiteford to LGAO, 23 Jan 1863.
61. P.R.O., MH 13, 145/727 Robert Morgan to Sir George Grey, 13 March 1865.
62. *The Times*, 2 Sept. 1881, 5.
63. P.R.O., MH 13, 144/541 William Eastlake to the GBH, 9 Jan 1855.
64. P.R.O., MH 13, 145/2492 Charles Whiteford to William Bruce, 27 May 1871; in 1866 the total revenue was £152,321—see P.R.O., MH 13, 145/1894 Charles Whiteford to Sir George Grey, 2 July 1866. Also W.D.R.O., P18/1196 Plymouth Rate Book, 1871.
65. P.R.O., HLG 2, 61/15230-58 Skardon to the Treasury, 23 Sept. 1858.
66. P.R.O., MH 13, 145/7936 Robert Morgan to the Home Office, 20 June 1871.
67. P.R.O., HLG 2, 62/1812-88 Walter Wilson to the Treasury, 28 Jan 1888.
68. P.R.O., HLG 2, 61/11046-65 Charles Whiteford to the Treasury, 7 July 1865.
69. P.R.O., HLG 2, 62/15420-70 C. Whiteford to the Treasury, 11 Aug 1870.

70. P.R.O., HLG 2, 62/15421-70 William Mortimer to the Treasury, 11 Aug 1870; also 102-71 William Mortimer to the Treasury, 29 Dec 1871.
71. P.R.O., HLG 2, 62/13380-87 Walter Wilson to the Treasury, 26 Aug 1887.
72. P.R.O., HLG 2, 62/144049-96 J.H. Ellis to Local Government Board, 5 Nov. 1896.
73. P.R.O., HLG 2, 62/443-98 Plymouth Corporation Management Scheme, 8 Jan 1898.
74. Sutcliffe 1982 (see note 1), 110.